BE
JOYFUL

50 Days to Defeat the Things That Try to Defeat You

Joyce Meyer

NEW YORK · NASHVILLE

FaithWords
Hachette Book Group
1290 Avenue of the Americas, New York, NY 10104
faithwords.com
twitter.com/faithwords

First Edition: May 2022

FaithWords is a division of Hachette Book Group, Inc. The FaithWords name and logo are trademarks of Hachette Book Group, Inc.

The publisher is not responsible for websites (or their content) that are not owned by the publisher.

The Hachette Speakers Bureau provides a wide range of authors for speaking events. To find out more, go to www.hachettespeakersbureau.com or call (866) 376-6591.

Library of Congress Cataloging-in-Publication Data
Names: Meyer, Joyce, 1943- author.
Title: Be joyful : 50 days to defeat the things that try to defeat you / Joyce Meyer.
Description: First edition | Nashville : FaithWords, 2022.
Identifiers: LCCN 2021053884 | ISBN 9781546029281 (hardcover) |
ISBN 9781546001072 (large type) | ISBN 9781546029298 (ebook)
Subjects: LCSH: Joy—Religious aspects—Christianity. |
Bible. Epistles of Paul—Theology.
Classification: LCC BV4647.J68 M48 2022 | DDC 241/.4—dc23/eng/20211130
LC record available at https://lccn.loc.gov/2021053884

ISBNs: 978-1-5460-2928-1 (hardcover), 978-1-5460-0107-2 (large type),
978-1-5460-2929-8 (ebook)

Printed in Canada

MRQ-T

10 9 8 7 6 5 4 3 2 1

BE
JOYFUL

CONTENTS

One of the most remarkable stories in the Bible is the account of the apostle Paul, previously known as Saul. As a young man, he was zealous in following the Jewish law—zealous to the point that he persecuted Christians. According to Acts 8:3, he "began to destroy the church. Going from house to house, he dragged off both men and women and put them in prison." Because of his hatred for followers of Christ, he was determined to stop the spread of the early church. In these activities, Saul truly believed he was serving God and doing the right thing. Later in his life, he realized that God had mercy on him because he was ignorant and lacked knowledge (1 Timothy 1:13).

Even though Saul did many wrong things, God, in His mercy, chose to visit him in an amazing way. According to Acts 9:1–2, while Saul "was still breathing out murderous threats against the Lord's disciples," he requested permission from the high priest to travel to Damascus, hoping to capture and jail more believers in Christ. Something shocking and wonderful happened during his trip:

> As he neared Damascus on his journey, suddenly a light from heaven flashed around him. He fell to

the ground and heard a voice say to him, "Saul, Saul, why do you persecute me?"

"Who are you, Lord?" Saul asked.

"I am Jesus, whom you are persecuting," he replied.

Acts 9:3–5

After this encounter, Saul became known as Paul. One of the lessons of Paul's miraculous conversion is that if God's grace can transform a persecutor of Christians into one of Christianity's greatest heroes, He can do *anything* for *anybody*. No matter what you need in your life, God can bring it to pass.

Paul's experience on the road to Damascus changed him completely—from a persecutor of Christians to a powerful minister of the gospel and writer of New Testament letters that have shaped Christian theology for centuries. Paul was forgiven and so transformed that after his personal encounter with Jesus, he forever turned his back on his old life and began pouring all of his passion and energy into helping others know Jesus and live victorious Christian lives.

One of the hallmarks of Paul's life and writings is his unbounded joy. In fact, he has been called "the apostle of joy." Joy is a fruit of the Holy Spirit (Galatians 5:22–23) and a quality that can range from extreme hilarity to calm delight. Because the Holy Spirit lives in us as believers, we can have and demonstrate joy in every circumstance we face. Anyone can be joyful when they have everything they want or when everything is going their way, but it takes the power of the Holy Spirit to remain steadfastly joyful in our hearts when we face difficulties or disappointments. Joy helps us enjoy life's happy seasons and gives us strength to persevere in faith and trust through hard times. According to Nehemiah 8:10, "The joy of the Lord is your strength." The more joyful you are, the stronger you will be.

Just as God met Paul on a journey and transformed him into a man of joy, I pray that God will meet you on the journey you will take through Paul's writings over the next fifty days as you gain strength to be joyful in every circumstance. These passages have changed my life, helped me mature in Christ, and taught me to find joy in each day, no matter what it may hold. I believe that they will do the same for you as you meditate on them and apply them to your life. I am praying for you, that as you go through this book God will use it to draw you into the joy that comes with a deeper, more intimate, and more powerful relationship with Him.

CHAPTER 1

Grace and Peace Lead to Joy

Galatians 1:3-5

Grace and peace to you from God our Father and the Lord Jesus Christ, who gave himself for our sins to rescue us from the present evil age, according to the will of our God and Father, to whom be glory for ever and ever. Amen.

Paul frequently opens his letters with "Grace and peace to you from God our Father and the Lord Jesus Christ." These words are not simply a salutation, but a beautiful and powerful blessing. This greeting was much more beneficial to the hearer than most of our greetings might be today. We may greet a person with "hello" or "hi," but in saying "Grace and peace to you…" Paul expresses his heartfelt wish for his readers to experience the power of amazing grace and the wonderful peace of God—"which transcends all understanding"—in their lives (Philippians 4:7).

As you and I begin this fifty-day journey together, I pray grace and peace for you, and I hope you will become increasingly aware of all the ways God's grace and peace will help you in every area of your life. I also pray that you will deliberately watch for Him to extend grace and peace to you, because when you look for them, you will see that He makes them available in more ways than you may have imagined.

> For the kingdom of God is not a matter of eating and drinking, but of righteousness, peace and joy in the Holy Spirit.
>
> Romans 14:17

Over the years I have come up with a personal description of grace. To me, grace is God's freely given, undeserved favor and power that enables us to do with ease what we could never do on our own with any amount of struggle or self-effort. We are saved by grace through faith in Jesus Christ (Ephesians 2:8), and we can live our everyday lives—caring for our families, running our households, fulfilling our job responsibilities, and doing everything else we do each day—by grace through faith. There are no limits to the ways we need God's grace, and, thankfully, there is no limit to the grace God is willing to give us. Jerry Bridges wrote in *The Discipline of Grace*— and I agree—that "Your worst days are never so bad that you are beyond the *reach* of God's grace. And your best days are never so good that you are beyond the *need* of God's grace."

Understanding and receiving God's grace makes it possible for us to live in peace. When I hear people say they have no peace in their lives, I feel sorry for them, because a life without peace is difficult, stressful, and joyless. Regardless of what else anyone may have—power, position, an excellent education, good looks, riches, an engaging personality, influential friends, possessions—it is worth nothing if they don't have peace to go along with it. In fact, all of these external things can become burdens when people do not have peace on the inside.

Grace leads to peace, and peace leads to joy. In fact, I don't think it's possible to be truly joyful if we are not living in God's grace and peace. When I use the word *joy* or *joyful*, I am not referring to what the world calls "happiness" or "happy." Happiness rises and falls, depending on the situations or moods in which people find themselves. But joy can stay steady through ups and downs, and despite what we would call a "bad mood." Joy is not determined by circumstances. It is a gift from God, and it follows a life of grace and peace. As an old spiritual says about joy, "The world didn't give it, and the world can't take it away."

God offers you grace and peace today and every day. When you live in Him, you have access to His grace and peace in every situation, which will lead you to great joy.

Things to Think About

1. How has receiving God's grace and peace brought joy to a specific situation in your life?
2. What circumstances are challenging your joy right now, and how can you receive God's grace and peace in them?

CHAPTER 2

The Fruit of the Holy Spirit

Galatians 5:22–23 AMPC

But the fruit of the [Holy] Spirit [the work which His presence within accomplishes] is love, joy (gladness), peace, patience (an even temper, forbearance), kindness, goodness (benevolence), faithfulness, gentleness (meekness, humility), self-control (self-restraint, continence). Against such things there is no law [that can bring a charge].

Joy is a fruit of the Holy Spirit, who lives in all believers. If Jesus Christ is your Lord and Savior, His Holy Spirit lives in you and gives you the ability to go through every situation with love, joy, peace, patience, kindness, goodness, faithfulness, gentleness (meaning humility), and self-control.

> As God's children, we have the Holy Spirit living inside us, and with Him come all the fruits of the Spirit, including joy.
>
> Joyce Meyer

You may notice that the first word in today's verse is *but*, which makes us wonder what came before it. The preceding verses list works of the flesh (life without God's guidance), which include "sexual immorality, impurity and debauchery; idolatry and witchcraft; hatred, discord, jealousy, fits of rage, selfish ambition, dissensions, factions and envy; drunkenness, orgies, and the like" (Galatians 5:19–21).

But there is an alternative to the kind of troubled, joyless life the works of the flesh lead to, and it is the fruit of the Holy Spirit. Let me encourage you to take a moment to think about the works of the flesh and then about the fruit of the Spirit. You have the freedom to choose how you want to live. I have chosen to live by the Spirit, and I hope you will too.

The fruit of the Spirit does not simply appear in your life when you become a Christian. It starts with a tiny seed that is planted when you give your life to Christ, and it develops over time, just as an apple or a pear would. The more you cultivate or practice it, the stronger and more mature it becomes.

The first word in the list of fruit is *love*, and the last word is *self-control*. This is important because we can cultivate all the fruit by focusing on love and self-control. Each fruit comes from love and is a form of love but is also held in place by self-control. Let me explain.

If you concentrate on developing the fruit of love, you will also demonstrate joy, peace, patience, kindness, goodness, faithfulness, and gentleness. At times, you may not feel like expressing these qualities, but self-control will enable you to show them. As an example, consider the fruit of patience. Let's say you love your teenage children with all your heart, but one day, they seem determined to do everything that exasperates you. Because you love God and you love them, you don't want to grow impatient, lose your temper, and say angry, hurtful words you would regret. How would you keep from doing that? Self-control. I think you can see exactly what I mean and can understand how the same principle would apply to the other fruit of the Spirit.

There are times in life when circumstances can be so difficult or sad that you think you cannot possibly be joyful. You may even wonder if you will ever experience joy again. These are the moments to exercise self-control and remind yourself that the joy of the Lord lives in you and that it is your strength. You can take joy in the fact that you know God, that He hears and answers prayer, that He cares for you, and that He will *never* leave you. Some seasons of life are happy and wonderful, and others are not. Happiness is a human emotion that often depends on circumstances, but joy is a fruit of the Holy Spirit—a quality that comes from your relationship with God. This is why every season of your life can have its unique joy, because the Holy Spirit lives in you.

Things to Think About

1. Think about the fruits of the Holy Spirit. Which one do you need to focus on today?
2. How can self-control help you grow in that fruit?

CHAPTER 3

The Importance of Helping Others

Galatians 6:2

Carry each other's burdens, and in this way you will fulfill the law of Christ.

One way the enemy tries to steal our joy is by trying to put more stress or pressure on us than we think we can bear. This could come through financial strain, the weight of knowing that an adult child struggles with addiction, needing to make a difficult decision, being treated unjustly, or countless other situations that are burdensome to us. When we try to carry heavy burdens in our own strength without God's grace, our hearts can grow heavy.

If you have ever carried a burden that simply seemed too much for you, then you can imagine how wonderful it would have been to have someone come alongside you to help you shoulder the load. I think Paul understood how difficult burden bearing can be, because he instructs us to "carry each other's burdens" (Galatians 6:2).

> I cannot even imagine where I would be today were it not for the handful of friends who have given me a heart full of joy.
>
> Charles R. Swindoll

Many people think the secret to joy lies in getting what they want. But I have learned that life's greatest joys are found in looking beyond ourselves and doing all we can to help others. One reason for this is that when others need help and get it, they feel joyful, relieved, grateful, and blessed. Any time you feel your joy level decreasing, do something for someone else, and pay attention to how much better you feel.

Paul's letter to the Galatians was intended to remind them that they were free from the ceremonial law of the Old Covenant, but in Galatians 6:2 he tells them to fulfill the new law of Christ, which is love, when he writes, "Carry each other's burdens, and in this way you will fulfill the law of Christ." This may seem contradictory, but it isn't. In today's passage, he is talking about fulfilling the moral law of love—loving one another, which is the new commandment Jesus gives (John 13:34). Our salvation doesn't depend on fulfilling this law, but our level of spirituality is evident by the fruit of love we display in our lives.

Christians are not promised lives without burdens, heartaches, and challenges. Many people struggle with worry, anxiety, fear, financial troubles, problems in relationships, depression, loneliness, illness, and countless other painful situations. We are to bear with them and help carry their burdens. This may mean listening, praying for them, making a phone call to check on them, running errands for them, helping them financially, or simply sitting with them as they grieve or wrestle with their situation. If you listen to them talk about what they are going through, you may easily discover a way you can help.

You may be in a season when life is good and you have no burdens, but there are people around you struggling under the weight of their burdens; it's important to remember them in prayer and offer to help them in practical ways.

At times, everyone needs help, and at times, everyone

can be a help to others. No one is too important to serve or help others. Paul says to resist selfish ambition and "in humility value others above yourselves" (Philippians 2:3). Although we are not to think of ourselves in downgrading or belittling ways, we are also to realize that in God's sight, our neighbors are just as valuable as we are.

Let's remember that although Jesus was "in very nature God," He took "the very nature of a servant" (Philippians 2:6–7). We can follow His example by also serving others, and one way to serve them is to help them carry their heavy loads. This will encourage them and bring joy to us.

Things to Think About

1. Who in your life could use your help to carry their burden right now?
2. In what specific ways can you help them?

CHAPTER 4

God Has Given You Every Spiritual Blessing

Ephesians 1:3

Praise be to the God and Father of our Lord Jesus Christ, who has blessed us in the heavenly realms with every spiritual blessing in Christ.

Today's verse gives us the good news that we have already been blessed with the spiritual blessings that are available from God, and this is certainly a reason to be joyful. Spiritual blessings are different from material blessings. A person may have great material wealth and be at the pinnacle of worldly success, yet be bankrupt in terms of spiritual blessings such as salvation, peace, joy, contentment, wisdom, fellowship with God, and true spiritual power.

God has provided for us everything we need, yet we often waste years trying to obtain things that mean much less than the spiritual blessings He has already given us because we are His children. All of these good blessings are available to us right now for us to possess, but we have to ask: Have we possessed our possessions? What I mean by this is that no matter what God has provided for us, His gifts don't help us unless we receive them by faith. We receive by faith through believing God's promises.

Joy is the simplest form of gratitude.

Karl Barth

For example, God has promised us wisdom and joy. Do you believe that you have wisdom? Do you believe that joy is already residing in your spirit, or are you trying to find joy in things that have no ability to ever give you true joy? When you believe you have something, you no longer look for it.

Let me explain further. I have a house, and it has a lot of great stuff in it. I also have a key to my house, which gives me access to everything inside of it. But if I don't use the key, then the belongings inside the house do me no good. The key to all the good things (spiritual blessings) God has already provided is the belief that they belong to us. We can live with a childlike faith that simply accepts what God says without needing physical proof of it. Hebrews 11:1 says, "Now faith is confidence in what we hope for and assurance about what we do not see."

The more we realize what God has already done for us through Jesus and the more we receive it by faith, the more we are able to find real joy in each day. Our true life is not found in our circumstances, but inside of us. Jesus says that the Kingdom of God is within us (Luke 17:21 AMPC). This means that we will never access spiritual blessings and the things of God by looking to external surroundings or resources; we will find them in our hearts.

Let me encourage you to get up each morning and think, *I have everything that I need to have a wonderful day. It is in my heart because through Christ, God has already blessed me with every spiritual blessing available.* You will find this kind of thinking to be much better than trying all day to find something to make you happy and then being disappointed because somehow what you thought you wanted evaded you once more, or you got what you wanted but it didn't make you happy like you thought it would. Start your day with this positive thought—*God has blessed me today*—and you'll find yourself more joyful all day long.

Things to Think About

1. What do you need to truly enjoy your life?
2. Have you "possessed the possessions" God has given to you?

CHAPTER 5

Knowing Who You Are in Christ

Ephesians 1:7-10

In him we have redemption through his blood, the forgiveness of sins, in accordance with the riches of God's grace that he lavished on us. With all wisdom and understanding, he made known to us the mystery of his will according to his good pleasure, which he purposed in Christ, to be put into effect when the times reach their fulfillment—to bring unity to all things in heaven and on earth under Christ.

Today's Scripture passage begins with the phrase "in him," meaning "in Christ." This important two-word phrase occurs often in the New Testament and represents a powerful spiritual truth that will raise your joy to a whole new level.

What does it mean to be "in him"? It means precisely this: God views those who, by faith, have received Jesus as their Savior as "in Christ," and because of this, all of God's wonderful promises are for us. We can take them personally and believe them for ourselves. Jesus sacrificed Himself for us so we could gain and experience God's blessings and goodness, and we receive them freely through our faith in Him.

> *Joy is the infallible sign of the presence of God.*
> Pierre Teilhard de Chardin

In a sense, as God's children we live in two places. The people to whom Paul wrote in Ephesians lived in the city of Ephesus, but he also wanted them to know that they lived in Christ. I live in St. Louis, Missouri, but I also live in Christ. Our natural life is lived with our feet on the ground, but simultaneously we have another life, a spiritual life in our hearts, and we live that life in Christ.

We reach a turning point in our lives as Christians when we realize who we are in Christ. I was a Christian for many years before I learned this truth. As a result, I lived in frustration and did not experience any practical victory in my daily life. Because I was a believer, I had God's promises of peace and joy, but because I did not know who I was in Christ, I often lived in inner turmoil and unhappiness.

Many Christians spend their lives trying to get things that already belong to them in Christ. For example, they may try to gain right standing with God through good works and behavior, yet they end up disappointed because they always fail. However, when they see the truth of the gospel and realize that because they are in Christ, God already views them as being in right relationship with Him (according to 2 Corinthians 5:21), their struggle ceases and joy increases. They can learn to rest in Christ's finished work at Calvary. While hanging on the cross, Jesus said, "It is finished" (John 19:30), and He meant that He had become the "atoning sacrifice" (payment) for all our sins—past, present, and future (1 John 2:2; 4:10). He fulfilled the law, and the door was now open for anyone who would believe to enjoy intimate, personal relationship with God.

You grow in the knowledge of who you are in Christ by studying God's Word and allowing it to transform your thinking. These ten Scripture-based confessions will help you become more established in what it means for you to be in Christ as you think about them, choose to believe them, and speak them aloud:

1. I am alive with Christ (Ephesians 2:5).
2. I am free from the law of sin and death (Romans 8:2).
3. I am holy and without blame before Him in love (Ephesians 1:4; 1 Peter 1:16).

4. I have the mind of Christ (1 Corinthians 2:16; Philippians 2:5).

5. I have the peace of God, which surpasses all understanding (Philippians 4:7).

6. I have the Greater One living in me; greater is He who is in me than he who is in the world (1 John 4:4).

7. I can do all things through Christ Jesus (Philippians 4:13).

8. I am a new creation in Christ (2 Corinthians 5:17).

9. I am more than a conqueror through Him who loves me (Romans 8:37).

10. I am the righteousness of God in Christ Jesus (2 Corinthians 5:21).

Things to Think About

1. Which truth mentioned above do you most need to become established in right now?

2. How can you demonstrate in practical ways that you believe this truth?

CHAPTER 6

Strength and Stability

Ephesians 3:16–17

I pray that out of his glorious riches he may strengthen you with power through his Spirit in your inner being, so that Christ may dwell in your hearts through faith.

In today's Scripture passage, Paul begins by praying for something many people need and pray for often: to be strengthened. In the Amplified Bible, this is also translated as being "spiritually energized" (3:16). We need strength and spiritual energy in all areas of our lives, yet the specific type of strength for which Paul prays is definitely the most important: strength in our inner self. When we speak of the inner self, we are referring to our inner being, which encompasses our thoughts, emotions, will, and conscience. Inner strength carries us through life's difficulties and challenges while allowing us to remain joyful.

We often pray for physical strength to be able to carry on with a project that has left us tired and fatigued or to get through a stressful situation. This is certainly appropriate and good, but strength in the inner self is even more valuable than natural energy and perseverance. When we are strong inwardly, that strength often manifests, or shows up, as determination that carries us through to victory in spite of many hardships.

> *The joy of the Lord is your strength.*
>
> Nehemiah 8:10

Being strengthened on the inside empowers us to be steadfast and stable, and one of the qualities that people in the world need to see in us is stability. A stable Christian is a great witness and example. If we are not stable on the inside and our temperament and commitment to

God changes constantly based on our circumstances, we don't inspire people to want to know Him. But if we remain emotionally steady through every situation, people notice. This stability comes from inner fortitude, not physical strength. As an example, think about this: No matter how many times a week people lift weights to build muscle, it will not help them be emotionally stable during hard times. Only God develops inner strength in us.

When you or someone you know is experiencing a great trial physically, mentally, emotionally, relationally, financially, or in any other way, the best way to pray is just as Paul did in this amazing prayer. Pray for inner strength and mighty power. Pray for the power of God to fill their (or your) innermost being through His Spirit.

The Amplified Bible indicates in Ephesians 3:16 that we are strengthened by the Holy Spirit "indwelling [our] innermost being and personality." Our personality is the way we express ourselves. Our thoughts and attitudes toward everything are expressed through our personality, and having a personality that is Spirit-filled sounds truly wonderful to me.

Just imagine how much better our relationships would be if we all had Spirit-filled personalities. This, of course, means that God and His ways could be seen in and through us daily as we interact with others. Surely, we can see the importance of this prayer Paul prayed in Ephesians 3:16–17. He was certainly led by the Holy Spirit in his praying.

If I had been praying for the people to whom Paul wrote in Ephesians, I might have prayed for them to be protected from difficulty and delivered from their trials, but Paul prayed something much better and much more valuable. Why pray for every little difficulty that comes our way to be removed? Would it not be better to pray that we would be so strong in our inner selves that we would barely even notice the hardships and certainly would not be affected by them? That way we could continue having peace and joy while walking in love toward others.

I pray often for inner strength, perhaps several times each day. I encourage you to begin to pray this important prayer also, both for yourself and for the people you love.

Things to Think About

1. Based on what you've learned from today's reading, why is inner strength so important?
2. In what specific areas of your life do you need to pray to grow in inner strength?

CHAPTER 7

Devote Yourself to Prayer

Colossians 4:2

Devote yourselves to prayer, being watchful and thankful.

One of the best ways to find and maintain joy in our lives is to devote ourselves to prayer. I think some people misunderstand what prayer really is, so I'd like to clear up a few misconceptions about it. First, prayer is not an obligation; it is the greatest privilege we have. Second, prayer is not a religious activity; it is a relational conversation. If we overspiritualize prayer and turn it into something it isn't, we will not want to pray. It does not require being in a certain place, assuming a certain posture, or using theological words in a certain tone of voice. Third, we don't have to pray for a specific length of time or at specific times of day. Prayer is simply talking with God and listening to Him as we would in a conversation with a friend. God is our friend, and He wants to interact with us just the way we are without our trying to seem "religious" or super spiritual. We may have special set-apart times for prayer, and that is good, but keep in mind that we can pray anywhere at any time. You may want to kneel when you pray, and if so, that is good, but you can also pray while taking a walk.

I like to teach people to pray their way through the day. Let prayer become like breathing. Each day, start a conversation with God about anything and everything. As you go about your day, simply talk with Him about everything that happens, about the people you encounter, about what you think and how you feel. There is nothing—*nothing*—that is off-limits with God. If something is on your mind, you can tell Him all about it. Prayer opens the door to the power of God and invites Him to change things and people. It opens doors you could never open, and it closes doors that would lead to something that is not good.

> Would we have our joy full, as full as it is capable of being in this world, we must be much in prayer.
> Matthew Henry, *Complete Commentary* (John 15:11)

Prayer is what changes our circumstances and our relationships, and it also changes us. It is amazing to pray and then watch God answer your prayers. It is one of my greatest joys in life.

There are many reasons to pray, but I want to focus on just one of them: God hears us and answers us when we pray. According to James 5:16, "The heartfelt and persistent prayer of a righteous man (believer) can accomplish much [when put into action and made effective by God—it is dynamic and can have tremendous power]" (AMP).

Some people are reluctant to pray because they do not think God will hear and answer them. Others hesitate to pray because they are independent and want to do things themselves. They fail to realize how much God loves and wants to help them. God is interested in everything that concerns us. No matter how tiny or seemingly unimportant it may be, if it concerns us, God is interested in it. If something hurts us, God wants to comfort us. If something is too hard for us, He wants to help. All we have to do is ask (James 4:2).

In today's verse, Paul teaches us not only to be watchful

but also to be thankful. Whenever we pray, we should do so with a thankful heart. We can thank God in advance for the way He will answer our prayers and for all the good things He has done in our lives. The more thankful we are, the more joyful we will be.

Things to Think About

1. What are some specific ways you might become more devoted to prayer?
2. Recall a time when God answered your prayer, and take a moment to thank Him again for doing that.

CHAPTER 8

The Joy of Being Rooted and Built Up in Christ, Part 1

Colossians 2:6-7

So then, just as you received Christ Jesus as Lord, continue to live your lives in him, rooted and built up in him, strengthened in the faith as you were taught, and overflowing with thankfulness.

Today and tomorrow, I'd like for us to focus on the idea of being "rooted and built up" in Christ, which leads to a life of ever-increasing faith, thankfulness, and joy. Just as a tree in the natural world can be strong because it is deeply rooted and built up, you and I can allow the roots of our lives to go deep in God, and that's what Paul is talking about in Colossians 2:6–7.

I like the way the Amplified Bible, Classic Edition renders Colossians 2:7 for several reasons. I'll explain one of those reasons today and the other two tomorrow. The verse reads:

> Have the roots [of your being] firmly and deeply planted [in Him, fixed and founded in Him], being continually built up in Him, becoming increasingly more confirmed and established in the faith, just as you were taught, and abounding and overflowing in it with thanksgiving.

One reason I appreciate this version of Colossians 2:7 is that it focuses on the inner life. When Paul writes in Colossians 2:7 about "the roots of your being," he is referring to the depth of the person we are on the inside. We all have an inner life and an outward life. The outward life is what we present to other people. It may include the way we dress or style our hair; our behavior; the car we drive or the house we live in; our education, job, hobbies, and interests; our natural gifts; the skills we develop; or our social networks and connections.

> *Happiness is the result of what happens of an agreeable sort. Joy has its springs down deep inside. And that spring never runs dry, no matter what happens. Only Jesus gives that joy.*
>
> S. D. Gordon

The inner life is what happens on the inside of us, where people cannot see it. It is its own world of thoughts, feelings, ideas, beliefs, and decisions. This is where our hearts are, and it is where we connect with God. In fact, the Bible says, "For behold, the kingdom of God is within you [in your hearts]" (Luke 17:21 AMPC). When we receive Christ as Lord and Savior, He comes to live on the inside of us by the Holy Spirit. His life within us ultimately transforms our outward life, but that transformation begins in our hearts.

A good life is not about what happens on the outside— our circumstances, or what people think of us, or how successful we seem to be by the world's standards. Many people today look only at the outside of other people's lives and decide that people who appear certain ways on the outside must have a "good life." The truth is, a good life is about what goes on inside of us.

I have learned that people can live under the best circumstances in the world but still be miserable if they have bad attitudes. If they think negatively, have negative emotions, or do not like themselves, they will still be unhappy.

On the other hand, people can face all kinds of challenges in their circumstances and still be joyful.

Many people in the world today are facing financial trouble, family problems, health challenges, and all kinds of struggles, yet they know and trust the Lord, and they find joy and strength in Him. With the right mindset, a happy heart, a good attitude, and the confidence that God loves you, your inner life can be strong, peaceful, and joyful. You can make it through life's tests and trials without feeling that they are major obstacles. Your trials may still pose challenges for you, but you do not have to be slowed down by poor attitudes, wrong thinking, or negative emotions that rob you of your joy.

Things to Think About

1. How does your personal inner life affect your outward life?
2. Think of someone who has stayed joyful in the midst of a very trying situation. How has their joy impacted you?

CHAPTER 9

The Joy of Being Rooted and Built Up in Christ, Part 2

Colossians 2:6-7

So then, just as you received Christ Jesus as Lord, continue to live your lives in him, rooted and built up in him, strengthened in the faith as you were taught, and overflowing with thankfulness.

Today I want to continue looking at the Amplified Bible, Classic Edition version of Colossians 2:7:

> Have the roots [of your being] firmly and deeply planted [in Him, fixed and founded in Him], being continually built up in Him, becoming increasingly more confirmed and established in the faith, just as you were taught, and abounding and overflowing in it with thanksgiving.

I mentioned yesterday that I appreciate this rendering of this verse because it focuses on the inner life. A second reason I like this verse is that it emphasizes what it means to be rooted in Christ by saying "deeply planted." Anything that is deeply rooted also becomes built up and strengthened.

The precepts of the Lord are right, giving joy to the heart.
Psalm 19:8

There is a big difference between things that have been shallowly planted and deeply planted. This is true in the natural world, and it is true in our spiritual lives. Think of it this way: I could dig a shallow hole in my yard and plant a small tree in it. But in a storm, the tree might be uprooted because its roots are too shallow. In contrast, if a fully grown oak tree had been in my yard for decades and its root system reached deep into the ground, I could be more confident that tree would withstand storms or strong winds.

The psalmist describes a deeply rooted person this way:

> Blessed is the one who does not walk in step with
> the wicked or stand in the way that sinners take or
> sit in the company of mockers, but whose delight
> is in the law of the Lord, and who meditates on
> his law day and night. That person is like a tree
> planted by streams of water, which yields its
> fruit in season and whose leaf does not wither—
> whatever they do prospers.
>
> Psalm 1:1–3

Notice that someone who is like a deeply rooted tree meditates on God's Word "day and night." To *meditate* on God's Word is to be like a cow chewing its cud—to chew on it and chew on it and chew on it. When you eat your food, chewing it well is important. If you don't, you will not get all the benefits of eating it. You can apply this idea to the way you approach God's Word. The way you meditate on the Word is to turn it over and over in your mind, thinking about it in depth, asking the Holy Spirit to reveal its meaning, and pondering how you can apply it to your life. The word *meditate* actually means "to confess or to mutter over and over," almost under your breath.

The idea of meditating on the Word connects to the third reason I appreciate the Amplified Bible, Classic Edition rendering of Colossians 2:7. It says we are to be "continually built up" in Christ and that we are "becoming increasingly more confirmed and established in the faith." We become more and more established in our faith by constantly reminding ourselves of what God's Word says, by studying it repeatedly, and by hearing and speaking it over and over again—as you just read about in Psalm 1:1–3.

No one has ever heard enough of God's Word. Everyone needs more and more of it, every day. It always strengthens us, always helps us, and always leads us to victory. I encourage you to study God's Word with enthusiasm, as though you are expecting to find a precious Bible gem that will help you greatly. Take each truth you study personally, as if the Holy Spirit inspired the writing of the Bible just for you.

Things to Think About

1. What can you do to grow in your faith and to become more deeply rooted in Christ?
2. How can being deeply rooted and built up in Christ increase your joy?

CHAPTER 10

How to Receive God's Blessings

Galatians 3:7-9

Understand, then, that those who have faith are children of Abraham. Scripture foresaw that God would justify the Gentiles by faith, and announced the gospel in advance to Abraham: "All nations will be blessed through you." So those who rely on faith are blessed along with Abraham, the man of faith.

Do you believe God wants to bless you beyond what you are currently experiencing? He does. That would certainly increase your joy, wouldn't it? He has many blessings in store for you, and though you may not yet possess all He ultimately wants to give to you, you can believe He will act at the proper time and in the right way. You can receive His blessings by faith and look forward to them.

How do we receive all that God has for us? We receive by faith, by having childlike trust that what God promises in His Word is true and that if we wait for it patiently, we will get it. No matter how long the blessings may take to manifest, we can wait with confidence, knowing that God will never leave us (Deuteronomy 31:8) and that "no matter how many promises God has made, they are 'Yes' in Christ. And so through him the 'Amen' is spoken by us to the glory of God" (2 Corinthians 1:20). We can say with the psalmist, "Those who know your name trust in you, for you, Lord, have never forsaken those who seek you" (Psalm 9:10).

As believers, our joy and peace are not based in doing and achieving, but in believing. Joy and peace come as a result of our relationship with the Lord.

Joyce Meyer

You may not be where you want to be right now in certain areas of your life, but you can be thankful that you are not where you once were. You are making progress, even if it is only a tiny bit at a time. Celebrate your victories and progress rather than mourn over your failures. Every step you take—even tiny ones—moves you closer to receiving more from God.

Paul reminds the Galatians that God promised Abraham that He would bless him, and that "those who have faith are children of Abraham" and "are blessed along with Abraham, the man of faith" (Galatians 3:7, 9). Jesus is a descendant of Abraham, and the blessings promised to him (Abraham) come to us through Jesus Christ because we are "those who have faith."

God's covenant with Abraham took place 430 years prior to the giving of the law to Moses. Abraham inherited by faith, but then Moses and the Israelites worked and struggled to keep the law. God's Word doesn't tell us that we inherit the blessings of Moses; it tells us we inherit the blessings of Abraham. God gave the law for one reason: to prove to humanity that we could not keep it and that we need a Savior. Jesus fulfilled the law in its entirety, and because we are in Him, we are free from all its rules and regulations, and we can live by grace through faith.

I want to bless my children and grandchildren in many ways, and all I want from them is their love, their respect, and some of their time. I think we can easily see that God wants the same from us. No one has seen or imagined all the good things that "God has prepared for those who love him" (1 Corinthians 2:9). Since this is true, it should be our privilege to give Him our love and worship and to spend time in His presence.

Abraham believed God, and his faith was counted to him as right standing with God (Galatians 3:6). You and I also have the amazing opportunity to believe God. Like Abraham, we can believe Him for what we cannot see, and we can wait confidently and in joyful expectation of all the blessings He wants to give us as His children.

Things to Think About

1. Do you believe God has blessings in store for you, far more than you are currently experiencing?
2. How are you exercising your faith for the blessings God wants to give to you?

CHAPTER 11

You're Adopted!

Galatians 4:4-7

But when the set time had fully come, God sent his Son, born of a woman, born under the law, to redeem those under the law, that we might receive adoption to sonship. Because you are his sons, God sent the Spirit of his Son into our hearts, the Spirit who calls out, "Abba, Father." So you are no longer a slave, but God's child; and since you are his child, God has made you also an heir.

In Galatians 4:4–5, Paul offers a succinct summary of why God sent His Son, Jesus, to earth: "to redeem those under the law, that we might receive adoption to sonship." To be adopted is to become a legal part of a family, with all the rights, privileges, and responsibilities of a biological child. This is the way God sees us—as His true sons and daughters. Paul continues in verses 6 and 7 by explaining that because we are God's children, the Holy Spirit lives in our hearts and bears witness (gives us confirmation or assurance) to the fact that God is our Father. And the good news goes on: As children of God, we do not relate to Him as slaves are subject to a taskmaster, but as sons and daughters relate to a loving Father. We know that we are God's children because the Holy Spirit causes our hearts to bear witness to this truth (Romans 8:15–16).

Under the Old Covenant (the former way of relating to God under the law), we were not redeemed or rightly related to God. People labored and worked hard to make themselves acceptable to God through keeping the Law of Moses. What a joyless, tiring existence! But under the New Covenant (the way of relating to God by grace through faith), we receive Jesus by faith. We are born again and made new (1 Peter 1:23; 2 Corinthians 5:17), and we have the ability to be led by the Holy Spirit, not by rules and regulations that direct us as we try to relate to God. He has redeemed us from all that the law required of us.

We become children and inheritors rather than laborers or servants. We have the right to a full inheritance, which God releases to us little by little as we grow spiritually.

Paul writes in greater depth about our position as heirs of God in Romans 8:14–17:

> *Simple, childlike believing releases the joy that is resident in our spirit because the Holy Spirit lives there.*
> Joyce Meyer, *The Confident Woman Devotional*

> For those who are led by the Spirit of God are the children of God. The Spirit you received does not make you slaves, so that you live in fear again; rather, the Spirit you received brought about your adoption to sonship. And by him we cry, "Abba, Father." The Spirit himself testifies with our spirit that we are God's children. Now if we are children, then we are heirs—heirs of God and co-heirs with Christ, if indeed we share in his sufferings in order that we may also share in his glory.

To be co-heirs with Christ means that we share His spiritual blessings and inheritance because of our faith in Him. Jesus says that everything the Father has is His, and all that is His is ours also (John 16:15). This gives me great joy, and I am sure it has the same impact on you. People who receive an inheritance typically are happy to get it, even though they have lost a loved one. As God's children, we can be sure that He will never leave us. He is always with us through the Holy Spirit, and He gives us an inheritance while also allowing us to enjoy His presence.

God brings us into His family because He *wants* to be our Father, not because of what we do or don't do. Only when we understand that we cannot do anything to make God love us or accept us and realize that we are saved and made right with God through Christ and Him alone can we truly live. Then we can experience life the way we should as children of God and enjoy the blessings He wants to give us as co-heirs with Christ.

Things to Think About

1. In your own words, why does being a child of God give you joy?
2. How does being a co-heir with Christ make a difference in your life?

CHAPTER 12

Righteousness Comes through Faith

Galatians 5:2–6

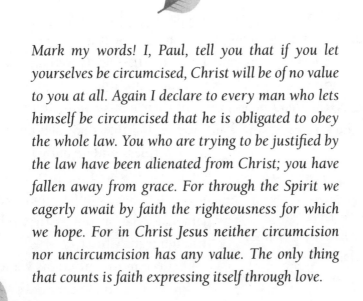

Mark my words! I, Paul, tell you that if you let yourselves be circumcised, Christ will be of no value to you at all. Again I declare to every man who lets himself be circumcised that he is obligated to obey the whole law. You who are trying to be justified by the law have been alienated from Christ; you have fallen away from grace. For through the Spirit we eagerly await by faith the righteousness for which we hope. For in Christ Jesus neither circumcision nor uncircumcision has any value. The only thing that counts is faith expressing itself through love.

The point of today's Scripture reading is this: No one can have self-righteousness and the righteousness of God through faith in Jesus at the same time. Once Jesus fulfilled the Old Testament law (Matthew 5:17), circumcision (the outward sign of belonging to God) was no longer necessary. We now enter into relationship with Him through placing our faith in Him and demonstrating that faith through our love for Him.

The Jews who read Paul's letter to the Galatians at the time must have struggled with today's passage, because it meant that their obedience to the Old Covenant law (including circumcision) meant nothing. For generations, they had been proud of their law-keeping and self-righteousness. Now, Paul was saying that their self-effort was worthless and actually problematic. It was holding them back from what they wanted: a close, personal relationship with God through Jesus Christ.

> Be rightly related to God, find your joy there, and out of you will flow rivers of living water.
>
> Oswald Chambers

I believe most Christians want to know that they can have a close, personal relationship with God and that He sees us as righteous—not as though something is wrong with us. Paul assures us of this in 2 Corinthians 5:21, which says that God made Jesus "to be sin for us, so that *in him we might become the righteousness* of God" (emphasis mine). We don't need to beg God to make us righteous. We can thank Him that He has *already* made us righteous because we are *in Christ*. This spiritual reality gives me great joy every day, and I pray that you will understand it and rejoice in it also.

Some people feel that God is angry with them, and they view their difficulties as God's discipline or punishment. This saddens me because it simply is not true. Yet I understand this way of thinking because, for many years, one question coursed through my mind almost constantly: *What's wrong with me?* And every time I made a mistake, I thought God was angry with me. I developed this incorrect way of thinking because my earthly father was angry and punished me often. When I came to know God personally, I carried that mindset into my relationship with Him. But God is nothing like human beings, nor does He think or behave as we do.

Please understand: God is not looking to punish you; Jesus satisfied completely all the punishment that our sins deserved through His death on the cross. He died for the sins we have already committed and for every sin we may commit in the future. His atonement covers them all! When we sin, all we need to do is repent and receive the forgiveness that is already ours because of Jesus' sacrifice on our behalf.

God does not want you to be afraid that He is angry with you or that He will punish you. The devil wants you to feel that way—to live in fear and be unhappy. But I want to make sure you know that you are not wrong with God; you

are made right with Him—and He sees you as righteous—
through the blood of Jesus Christ.

Being right with God through Christ does not mean you
do everything right all the time. No one does. But there is
a difference between your *who* and your *do*. *Who you are* in
Christ and *what you do* as a flawed human being are two
different things. That's good news!

Things to Think About

1. Why does the fact that you are righteous before God
   through Christ bring you joy?
2. In your own words, explain why this idea is important in your life: "There is a difference between your
   who and your *do*."

CHAPTER 13

No Turning Back

Galatians 4:8-9

Formerly, when you did not know God, you were slaves to those who by nature are not gods. But now that you know God—or rather are known by God—how is it that you are turning back to those weak and miserable forces? Do you wish to be enslaved by them all over again?

After the Galatians came to know God in a personal way, they were tempted to abandon their walk of faith and return to their old way of life. In today's passage, Paul is shocked that they could even consider returning to a life of bondage to rules and regulations, now that they had come to know God.

I am also shocked that anyone would think about returning to their old life once they have known God. My life prior to knowing Him intimately was characterized by fear, shame, bondage, and a measure of legalism (thinking I had to obey all the Christian "rules" to get God to love me). But once I came to know Him, my life changed completely. He brought me out of my negative ways and into a personal relationship with Him. I came to know true joy for the first time in my life when I entered into a close, personal relationship with God through Jesus Christ.

> The joy of the Lord will arm us against the assaults of our spiritual enemies, and put our mouths out of taste for those pleasures with which the tempter baits his hooks.
> Matthew Henry, *Complete Commentary* (Nehemiah 8:9-12)

Now, because I have enjoyed a long-term intimate relationship with Jesus, I often wonder why anyone would even want to get out of bed in the morning if they do not know Him. It seems to me that my life would be completely devoid of peace, joy, and meaning if I did not know God and live to serve Him.

Paul reminds the Galatians of what their lives were like prior to knowing God and being known by Him. True Christianity is not based on knowing *about* God, but on *knowing* God. It is having an intimate personal relationship with Him through Jesus Christ and being transformed into His image. To know God means to know and personally experience His character, which includes qualities such as His love, goodness, grace, mercy, forgiveness, righteousness, peace, joy, holiness, and many other wonderful attributes.

Paul also mentions being known *by* God, and this is as wonderful as knowing God. We all want to be known completely by someone who will accept and love us as we are. God knew us before the foundation of the earth was created. He saw our future even before we were born, and He has written down every day of our lives. He knows every thought we think before we think it and every word we will speak before we say it. Our Father not only knows us better than anyone else does, but He knows us even better than we know ourselves. There is no point in trying to hide anything from Him, because He already knows it. With God, we don't need to pretend, hide, or make excuses.

Jesus told His disciples that He chose them; they did not choose Him (John 15:16). This does not mean that we have no free will and are compelled to serve God, but it means that everything starts with God. We cannot come to Him unless He draws us.

No matter where you are on your spiritual journey—whether you are just starting out and have many questions about God or you have walked with God for decades and feel closer to Him now more than ever—let me encourage you to keep moving forward with Him. I hope you will never consider going back to the way you lived before you knew Him or giving up on Him. He will never give up on you, and no one will ever know you or love you like He will. This is a good reason for great joy.

Things to Think About

1. In what ways has knowing God and knowing that God knows you completely made a difference in your life and given you joy?
2. Think about your life before you knew God. Why would you not want to go back to that?

CHAPTER 14

Stay Free

Galatians 5:1

It is for freedom that Christ has set us free. Stand firm, then, and do not let yourselves be burdened again by a yoke of slavery.

There's no doubt about it: The more God sets us free, the more joyful we are. Have you ever achieved freedom in a certain area of your life and later found yourself trapped in that same situation all over again? Or have you seen this happen to a friend or family member? Perhaps you were once in bondage to debt, and you finally paid off all your bills, but then a year later, the debt had piled up once more. Or maybe you spent years in bondage to emotional eating and ended up overweight. You worked hard to stop eating when you were fearful or upset, you lost weight, and you felt much better. But then something extremely stressful happened, and your emotions drove you to overeat again.

People can be in bondage to all kinds of things, and they can feel like slaves to these habits, addictions, and mindsets. Any time someone breaks free from bondage and then falls back into it for some reason, it can be very discouraging. Today's Scripture passage is meant to strengthen and encourage us to keep the freedom God gave us.

Freedom can be difficult to gain, and sometimes even more difficult to maintain. If we want to *stay* free after we *get* free, we have to work at it. This is why Paul says to "stand firm." It means we will be tempted to let our freedom slip away, so we must intentionally guard against that.

If someone you love has gained

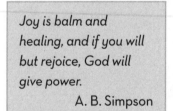

Joy is balm and healing, and if you will but rejoice, God will give power.

A. B. Simpson

freedom over something that held them captive for a long time and you see them slipping back into their old ways, you would want to plead with them, "Stop it! Don't go there! Don't do that to yourself again!" You would beg them to do whatever it takes to maintain their freedom. The same is true for you if you are that person slipping back into old patterns—you would want someone to plead with you to stay the course.

This is how Paul, desperate to see the Galatians stay free, felt about them. They had been living free from the law, and he urged them to maintain the freedom they had enjoyed. They had been delivered not only from their sins but also from the rules and regulations of the Old Covenant law. As Gentiles, they had not lived under the law of the Old Covenant, but I am sure that as idol worshippers they were very familiar with the legalistic trappings of any religion without Jesus as its center. They certainly were accustomed to making sacrifices to appease the gods they assumed were angry, especially if anything in their circumstances was not good.

Now, they were in great danger of falling back into the bondage of legalism—being motivated to perform certain actions because they feared displeasing God if they didn't follow religious rules and make sacrifices for their sins. God doesn't want us to serve Him out of fear of His anger but because of our love and appreciation for all He has done and continues to do for us.

Believers in the one true God can now walk as they have never walked before. This was true for the Galatians, and it is true for you and me. We are no longer under the law, but we have the great privilege of being invited to follow the Holy Spirit rather than doing as we please, according to our fleshly desires. Through the power of the Holy Spirit, we can live holy, righteous lives and glorify God. He has set us free, and He empowers us to stay free. When we are free from bondage, we can live in peace and joy.

Things to Think About

1. In what ways has Christ set you free? How has that freedom increased your joy?
2. When you are tempted to fall back into old bondages, how can you stand strong against the temptation?

CHAPTER 15

Rejoice in the Lord

Philippians 3:1

Further, my brothers and sisters, rejoice in the Lord! It is no trouble for me to write the same things to you again, and it is a safeguard for you.

As I wrote in the introduction to this book, Paul can be considered the "apostle of joy." In addition, Philippians is considered the "epistle of joy." In today's verse, Paul reminds his readers to rejoice in the Lord. He never says that we can rejoice in our circumstances at all times, but that we can rejoice *in the Lord* at all times.

What does it take to rejoice in the Lord? It requires thinking about what we have in Christ rather than focusing on our circumstances. It also requires focusing on what we do have instead of what we do not have. We can rejoice because we have been forgiven of all our sins, our names are written in the Lamb's Book of Life, we have a personal relationship with God, and we will live in God's presence eternally. No matter what we do not have, we always have hope, and hope is powerful. We also have God's unconditional love, His strength, His peace, His grace, and a host of other wonderful blessings that would make a list too long to put in this book. These are all reasons to rejoice. In addition, God's Word contains more than five thousand promises, and surely that is cause for rejoicing.

Our thinking is the foundation for all of our emotions, and if we desire to have pleasant feelings such as joy and peace,

> It is not only a Christian's privilege, but also his duty to rejoice constantly in the Lord.
>
> H. A. Ironside, *Notes on the Epistle to the Philippians*

we need to think thoughts that produce them. Here is one great promise of God that causes me to rejoice: "And we know that in all things God works for the good of those who love him, who have been called according to his purpose" (Romans 8:28).

The Philippian believers to whom Paul writes faced a great possibility of the same types of persecution—and even death—that threatened him and others in the early church. Although Paul knew that they might endure hardship because of their faith, he also knew that their faith gave them many reasons to rejoice. For example, as he writes in Romans 8:35–39, *nothing* could separate them from the love of God found in Christ Jesus. This is a powerful thought and a reason for great joy.

Over the years, my speaking schedule has required me to travel a great deal, and Dave and I have experienced many inconvenient and irritating circumstances during that time. For example, during one heavy travel season, twice in one month the water went off on the floor of the hotel where our room was located. What are the chances that such an unusual occurrence would happen two times in one month in two different hotels? It's not likely, so we decided the enemy was merely trying to irritate us, and we refused to be irritated. I laughed and said, "If the water doesn't come back on by seven a.m., I will have to find another room in the hotel where I can get ready for the day. I cannot go to a conference looking the way I do, without the opportunity to clean up and fix my hair." I prayed, asking God to somehow solve the problem with the water by seven a.m., and at 6:55 a.m., an engineer knocked on the door to tell us the water was back on.

Perhaps if we prayed and kept our joy instead of becoming upset and losing it, we would see more amazing answers to prayer. Just as we can walk to a sink and choose to turn on the water, we can turn on our joy by deciding to have godly perspectives of our circumstances. Choose to rejoice today!

Things to Think About

1. Stop and think about some of the blessings in your life. How can you grow in your ability to rejoice in them?
2. In what situations can you choose to be joyful today?

CHAPTER 16

The Joy of Being in God's Will

Colossians 1:1

Paul, an apostle of Christ Jesus by the will of God, and Timothy our brother.

Colossians 1:1 is a short verse, but it is packed with meaning. Notice that Paul says he is an apostle "by the will of God." This is important because, as Christians, we want to follow God's will, and doing so gives us great joy. If we don't believe that the things we are doing are in God's will for us, how can we ever do them well or enjoy them?

When I teach about being in God's will, people often ask, "How can I know if I am walking in God's will for my life?" Here are two simple ways.

1. You will enjoy it.

John 10:10 tells us that Jesus came so that we may "have and enjoy life, and have it in abundance [to the full, till it overflows]" (AMP). God's will for you will not cause you to be miserable or excessively stressed. You may face challenges as you pursue it, but if it is God's will for you, He will give you the wisdom and grace to overcome any difficulty, and you will find joy in doing it.

> Joy is the holy fire that keeps our purpose warm.
> Helen Keller

2. You will be equipped for it.

I also believe that when we are in God's will, we will be good at what we are doing. God gives us the skills, gifts, and abilities to fulfill His will for our lives. He does not call us to do something without equipping us for it.

You may have to work, study, or prepare in some other way to carry out His call on your life, but you will have an aptitude for it and feel at ease in it. I have become very comfortable doing what I do as a teacher of God's Word. I have had to learn some lessons about doing it effectively, and I do work at it, but what I do is not hard for me because I am walking in God's will as I do it.

Finding God's will for your life is not difficult: You step out and try things until you find what is comfortable for you. *Comfortable* doesn't necessarily mean easy. You will likely have to work at it, but you will know in your heart that it is what you are supposed to be doing, and it will bring you peace and joy. If God calls you to do something, He will also provide what you need to do it—skills, finances, and, if necessary, people to help you, along with other resources.

As you seek to discover God's will for your life, you'll need to take some chances and walk by faith. If you try something you think may be God's will for you and you realize it isn't, simply change direction without getting frustrated or feeling condemned. Trust God to guide you to the next opportunity, and keep experimenting until you land in the place you know in your heart that God has for you. What He has for you may not look like what He has for other people, and that is okay. He has a unique purpose for everyone, and all you need to do is discover and fulfill the one He has for you without comparing yourself to others or trying to compete with them. Pursue His will for you wholeheartedly, regardless of what anyone else is doing, because that is where you'll find your joy.

The key lesson of Colossians 1:1 is to be sure you believe to the best of your ability that whatever you are doing is God's will for you at any given time in your life. Over the course of your life, certain things may change. God's will for you today may not be His will for you ten years from now, but as you continue to seek it, He will continue to reveal it.

Things to Think About

1. Do you believe that what you are doing right now reflects God's will for your life?
2. How have you reached that conclusion?

CHAPTER 17

The Blessings of Spiritual Maturity

Galatians 4:1–3

What I am saying is that as long as an heir is under-age, he is no different from a slave, although he owns the whole estate. The heir is subject to guardians and trustees until the time set by his father. So also, when we were underage, we were in slavery under the elemental spiritual forces of the world.

If parents die and leave an inheritance to their sons or daughters who are underage, the children will be provided for through their parents' will. But because the heirs are young, even though they have inherited an entire estate, they still function as children, which is not much different from functioning as servants. If the estate is run by hired help, they may in fact be cared for and expected to live in obedience to the household servants, who often have more authority than the underage children do.

The children have an inheritance and will receive it at the proper time, but until they mature, the resources their parents set aside for them will be administered by trustees. Had the parents not made this provision, the young people could have wasted their inheritance and perhaps brought shame on the family name due to their immaturity and youth.

> There is no greater joy in the Christian life than to trust Him and need no explanation.
> Jack Hyles

Our Father God views us as His sons and daughters. Jesus, His firstborn Son, has inherited everything the Father has, and we are joint heirs with Him through faith (Romans 8:17). God wants to bless us in countless ways, but in His wisdom, He does not release certain blessings and gifts to us until He knows we are mature enough to handle them.

It is my great delight to teach believers how to mature

so they may enjoy the life Jesus died to give them. Part of spiritual maturity is moving from a slave or servant mentality to the mentality of a child and an heir of God. This involves understanding that we are no longer subject to the law (rules and regulations that we think will make us acceptable to God), but that we now live under God's grace.

Think of it this way: Children live under rules to keep them going in the right direction, but as they mature, they learn to follow their father's heart, and the rules they have previously lived under are lifted. When my children were young, they each had a list of chores they were expected to do as part of the family. As they matured, they no longer needed the lists because they knew in their hearts what to do.

Thankfully, Jesus has set us free from the law. He says in John 8:36, "If the Son sets you free, you will be free indeed." How does this freedom manifest in our lives? Jesus gives us the answer in John 8:31–32. He says that as we hold to His teaching, we are His disciples, and we will know the truth, and the truth will set us free. The Amplified Bible helps us understand what it means to hold to His teaching by rendering John 8:31 this way: "If you abide in My word [*continually obeying My teachings and living in accordance with them*, then] you are truly My disciples" (emphasis mine).

God's Word is truth (John 17:17), and as we learn and follow it, we experience greater levels of freedom and joy. Paul writes that when he was a child, he behaved in childish ways, but when he became a man, he put aside those childish ways (1 Corinthians 13:11). I believe all Christians need to make a priority of becoming more and more spiritually mature. This will deepen our walk with God, make us better witnesses for Him, and help us enjoy the blessings and the inheritance He desires to give us.

Things to Think About

1. Why is it important for us not to receive certain blessings before we are mature enough to handle them?
2. In what ways have you personally experienced freedom through God's truth?

CHAPTER 18

Keep Running the Good Race

Galatians 5:7–8

You were running a good race. Who cut in on you to keep you from obeying the truth? That kind of persuasion does not come from the one who calls you.

> The Lord gives His people perpetual joy when they walk in obedience to Him.
>
> Dwight L. Moody

When Paul writes that the Galatians "were running a good race," he means that they were doing well in their lives as believers in Christ, but now they have allowed themselves to be deceived by false teaching and have fallen back into their old ways. Their previous enthusiasm, commitment, and love had weakened, and this damaged their reputation.

The Galatians began to backslide because of the lie that although they had been justified by faith in Jesus, they also needed to follow the law in order to be sanctified (made holy). Many people today also believe faith involves Jesus plus something else—such as church attendance or a certain amount of time in Bible study each day. While these activities do enhance the Christian experience when done by *grace*—not as rules or obligations—none of them affects God's love for us. Our faith in Jesus is enough. We need nothing else to be assured of God's love and acceptance. Paul mentions this more than once in Galatians, perhaps because it is such a temptation for many people.

This reminds me of the story of a rich man who asked Jesus what he must do to inherit eternal life (Mark 10:17–22). Jesus said to keep the commandments, and then He listed them. The young man responded that he had kept them all. Jesus, loving him, replied, "One thing you lack…Go, sell everything you have and give to the poor, and you will have treasure in heaven. Then come, follow me" (Mark 10:21).

Several things about this story stand out to me. First, Jesus loved the young man, so we can assume that everything He told him was intended to help him. Second, although the young man had done many good works, he still lacked one thing. We all lack something if we depend on our good works to justify us and give us entrance into eternal life. Jesus asked the man to give away all he had to the poor, but "he went away sad" (Mark 10:22). This occurred because money meant too much to him, and Jesus was trying to help him realize that. I believe that had the young man obeyed Jesus, he would have received in return much more than he gave away. I am certain that many go away "sad," as the young man did, because they are unwilling to obey God.

Overhearing this conversation, Peter commented to Jesus, "We have left everything to follow you!" (Mark 10:28). Jesus' response is good news for all of us: "Truly I tell you…no one who has left home or brothers or sisters or mother or father or children or fields for me and the gospel will fail to receive a hundred times as much in this present age: homes, brothers, sisters, mothers, children and fields—along with persecutions—and in the age to come eternal life" (Mark 10:29–30).

Jesus' words teach us that we don't have to wait until we get to heaven to receive a reward. Jesus did tell His disciples that they would be persecuted while on this earth, but He also said they would be blessed. This doesn't necessarily mean that the man would end up richer than he had been. He might have, if the Lord knew that would be best for him. It simply means that he would have had plenty of all that he needed, with peace and joy and all the other spiritual benefits that come with fully obeying God.

Things to Think About

1. Are you tempted to believe that God's love and acceptance depend on Jesus plus something else? Ask the Holy Spirit to strengthen you against that temptation.

2. What benefits have you received because you obeyed God?

CHAPTER 19

Sow Good Seeds

Galatians 6:7-8

Do not be deceived: God cannot be mocked. A man reaps what he sows. Whoever sows to please their flesh, from the flesh will reap destruction; whoever sows to please the Spirit, from the Spirit will reap eternal life.

Paul shares an important spiritual truth in today's Scripture passage, which is that God cannot be mocked and His principles cannot be set aside. He urges his readers not to be deceived into thinking we can behave badly and have good results. We reap what we sow.

I personally love this biblical truth because it lets me know that I have a measure of control regarding the way my life turns out. Look down the road and ask yourself what you want your life to look like in the future. Then be smart enough to realize that the harvest you will reap tomorrow will directly relate to the seeds you sow today.

> *Joy is a choice. A genuine spirit of joy does the heart good and it's truly contagious.*
> Charles R. Swindoll

We can see the principle of sowing and reaping easily when we think about gardening. We cannot sow onion seeds and reap tomatoes. We must sow the seed now that will produce the fruit or vegetable we desire to enjoy later.

God tells us in Genesis 8:22 that as long as the earth remains there will be "seedtime and harvest." If you are not satisfied with your harvest, perhaps you should consider the seed you have been sowing. For example, no one can sow anger and reap peace, nor can a person sow a bad attitude and reap a happy, joyful outlook on life.

If people have no friends or find that when they make new friends the friendships never last long, they would be wise to ask themselves how they treat their friends. Are they easy to get along with? Do they try to give others unwanted advice too often? Do they always wait for the other person to pay the bill when they share a meal together? People who are good friends always have plenty of friends.

If we sow mercy in our dealings with people, we will receive mercy from people who deal with us (Matthew 5:7). If we sow judgment toward others, we will receive judgment against ourselves; if we give, it will be given to us (Luke 6:37–38). We often focus on our harvest, but perhaps we should pay more attention to our seed.

Paul says that if we sow to the flesh, we will reap from the flesh. The Amplified Bible, Classic Edition adds that if we sow to the flesh, we will reap from the flesh "decay and ruin and destruction," but if we sow to the Spirit, we will reap life (Galatians 6:8). To sow to the flesh means to behave in a carnal manner, obeying the impulses of the flesh rather than following the guidance of the Holy Spirit; it means doing what we want to do rather than doing the will of God.

Saul was a king who did not fully obey God, and he ultimately lost his kingdom as a result (1 Samuel 15:22–28). Our actions bring consequences, good or bad. A person may live like there is no tomorrow, but tomorrow always comes, and with it comes the harvest of the seeds we have sown in the past.

On occasion, we do, of course, find ourselves confronted by problems we cannot avoid that come from the devil or merely from living in the world; nor do we always sow some specific bad seed that has caused them. But when we look at the aspects of our life we can influence by sowing good seeds, we should be diligent to do so, knowing that our efforts will be ultimately rewarded.

Things to Think About

1. Have you ever noticed in your own life or in someone else's life the relationship between sowing and reaping? What happened in that situation?
2. How can you sow good seeds today for the future you want to enjoy tomorrow?

CHAPTER 20

Patience and Joy

Colossians 1:9–12 **NKJV**

For this reason we also, since the day we heard it, do not cease to pray for you, and to ask that you may be filled with the knowledge of His will in all wisdom and spiritual understanding; that you may walk worthy of the Lord, fully pleasing Him, being fruitful in every good work and increasing in the knowledge of God; strengthened with all might, according to His glorious power, for all patience and longsuffering with joy; giving thanks to the Father who has qualified us to be partakers of the inheritance of the saints in the light.

I want to encourage you to read today's passage slowly and carefully. Notice how Paul prays for the Colossian believers. His prayer here, as well as his prayers throughout his letters, focuses on the inner life and on the readers' spiritual growth and relationship with God. When I first noticed the way Paul prayed, it transformed the way I pray. Until then, I did not think much about praying for my inner life. I now know that when we are strong on the inside, everything in our outer life falls into place. Inner strength is much more important than having things go exactly as we would like. I'm sure you know by now that everything in life will not always go as you would like them to. Life does have challenges, and when we face them, being strong and stable on the inside equips us to trust God and rely on His grace in the midst of them.

> God is bringing you into a whole new, fresh way of thinking, believing, and responding to life; and with that new way comes incredible joy and freedom. You will spend eternity walking in this kind of joyfulness. Why not start now?
>
> Jane Hansen Hoyt, *The View from Above*

When we study Paul's prayers, we notice his perspective on life's difficulties. He never prayed for his readers to avoid problems or for their problems to go away. I would summarize or paraphrase his prayers by saying he prayed that those who read his letters—including you and me—would endure their hardships with strength, faith, patience, and trust in God, and that they would persevere through trials with joy (Colossians 1:9–12; 2 Thessalonians 1:2–5).

I especially like the way the Amplified Bible, Classic Edition renders Colossians 1:11: "[We pray] that you may be invigorated and strengthened with all power according to the might of His glory, [to exercise] every kind of endurance and patience (perseverance and forbearance) with joy."

In all my years of ministry, I cannot remember even one time when someone asked me to pray that they would endure their difficulties with joy. Many people, however, have asked me to pray that they would be delivered from their problems. While no one is happy about the troubles they face, Paul teaches us that we can be joyful in the midst of them.

While God is certainly able to change our circumstances, He is interested in changing *us*. He does not enjoy seeing us struggle or suffer, but He does delight in our spiritual growth, and He uses our circumstances for good purposes. If we are honest with ourselves, we will probably admit that we have gained more inner strength and experienced more spiritual maturity through the hard times in our lives than through the easy ones.

Problems and difficulties are not fun, but they do strengthen us. They stretch our faith, they teach us to trust

God instead of relying on our own knowledge or resources (Proverbs 3:5–6), and they develop our compassion toward others when they encounter hardships.

We can see from today's passage that Paul believes there is a connection between trials, patience, and joy. The apostle James seems to believe the same way and clearly says we are to view our trials as "all joy" because they produce patience, and when patience is fully developed in us, we will lack nothing (James 1:2–4 NKJV).

Let me encourage you to pray Colossians 1:9–12 for yourself today. Then ask the Holy Spirit to lead you to pray it for several other people. Learn to pray without constantly asking God to take away your problems, but ask Him to help you and those for whom you pray to endure whatever you face with patience and joy, trusting Him to ultimately bring good from it.

Things to Think About

1. What have you learned about prayer from Colossians 1:9–12?

2. How will the lessons you have learned from today's passage and message change the way you pray about a certain trial you are currently facing—or change the way you will pray in the future?

CHAPTER 21

Top Priority

Colossians 1:18

And he is the head of the body, the church; he is the beginning and the firstborn from among the dead, so that in everything he might have the supremacy.

As "the head of the body," Christ is over and above everything. He is in control, and we are to follow His instructions and example. As long as the body takes direction from the head, we will be able to live peaceful, joyful, purpose-filled lives. But when the body starts trying to be in control, things become disorderly, confusing, and unstable.

Even though Christ is the head and we look to Him to know what to do, we still have free will. God always allows us to choose whether or not we will follow Him. If we decide to follow Christ, we also take on certain responsibilities. Our primary responsibility is to mature spiritually and demonstrate the resurrection life Jesus offers us, which Paul writes about in Philippians 3:10 when he mentions knowing Christ and "the power of his resurrection." This means you can be on earth in your physical body, going to work, going home, doing the dishes, cutting the grass, and going through everything that everyone else experiences, and still live in the power that Christ's resurrection offers you. Having the resurrection life that's available through Christ does not mean you will never have problems. It simply offers you a place in Christ where you can rise above the storms of

> You make known to me the path of life; you will fill me with joy in your presence, with eternal pleasures at your right hand.
>
> Psalm 16:11

life, maintain your joy in God, and refuse to give up your hope because you know that Christ, as the head, is in control of everything.

To relate to Jesus as our head means to give Him first place in our lives. If we do not give Him top priority, then whatever we do put in first place will become an idol to us, and it will fight to stay there. All sorts of things can become idols if we let them—even things that are good and noble, such as family, working hard, friends, or even serving God in ministry.

Many years ago, the ministry I was trying to build—the ministry God gave me—became more important to me than God. I did not mean for that to happen, but it did. I was so proud of myself and thought I was doing so well in life. But one day, God showed me that I was proud of myself because I was working for me. The problem was that I was not spending any time with Him. That was an important lesson for me to learn, and I have never forgotten it.

Nothing is more important than your relationship with God. Keep Him first in all things, and everything else will fall into its proper place. When we put Jesus first, we acknowledge that He is the head and we are part of the body, and we surrender everything about ourselves to Him. This idea makes some people nervous because they are afraid that if they put Jesus first, they may have to give up something very important to them. But Psalm 37:4 says: "Take delight in the Lord, and he will give you the desires of your heart." I can personally assure you that if you put

Jesus first, you will be amazed how much God will do for
you. His joy and peace will fill your heart, and you will
receive the desires of your heart in God's perfect timing.
This doesn't mean you won't have challenges, but you will
be able to overcome them by the power of the Holy Spirit
and live your life by His grace.

Things to Think About

1. Have you surrendered everything to God, giving
   Him top priority in your life? If not, what do you
   need to surrender?
2. If someone were to follow you around for a week,
   would that person know that God is your top priority? Why or why not?

CHAPTER 22

Working Out What God Has Put into Us

Philippians 2:12

Therefore, my dear friends, as you have always obeyed—not only in my presence, but now much more in my absence—continue to work out your salvation with fear and trembling.

Although Paul teaches that salvation is by grace alone, apart from works (Ephesians 2:8–9), he also tells us in today's verse to work out our own salvation. This means to get it from our hearts (spirits) into our everyday lives, so that we live as people who are saved, forgiven, and in relationship with God through Jesus Christ. The simplest way I know to explain this is to say that Paul is not speaking of *working for* salvation but of *working it out* with the help of the Holy Spirit.

We cannot work out what has not been worked into us. God gives us everything we need to be fruitful, peace-filled, joyful, mature believers at the time of our new birth—the moment when we believe that Jesus paid for our sins, died on our behalf for the forgiveness of our sins, and gave us the gift of life eternal. The new birth also includes our decision to believe that He triumphantly rose from the dead and is now seated in heavenly places waiting for the right time to return and bring our complete redemption.

> *Through the Spirit, the risen and glorified Lord will Himself take up residence in our cold hearts, and with Him comes His joy.*
> Catherine Marshall,
> *The Helper*

When we are born again, we are given the nature of God (1 John 3:9 AMPC), the fruit of the Holy Spirit (Galatians 5:22–23), right standing with God through Christ (2 Corinthians 5:17, 21), and many other wonderful blessings. These gifts are deposited into our spirits but need to be worked into our souls (our minds, wills, and emotions) and ultimately demonstrated through our physical bodies.

It is important for us to believe that God has given us all we need in order to do everything He asks of us. His provision comes as seed, for Christ is the "Seed" of God (Galatians 3:16–19 AMPC); as we work with the Holy Spirit, who waters the seed by teaching us and training us in the Word of God, helping us understand and apply it to our lives, this seed grows into the fullness of what He desires us to become. The more we become who He intends for us to be, the more our joy, satisfaction, and sense of purpose increase.

This is an important spiritual principle, because when we do not understand it, we struggle through life trying to become what we already are in Christ. When we are born again, God the Father, Jesus the Son, and the Holy Spirit come to dwell inside of our human spirit. He moves in, we might say, and makes His home in our hearts. And He has promised to never leave us or forsake us (Hebrews 13:5). He is with us always! We are spiritual beings who have a spirit, a soul, and a body. We need our bodies in order to dwell in this earth, and what we do in the body is what other people see.

Sometimes, when people are corrected, they say, "But my heart was right!" They wanted to do the right thing, and while that is commendable, it should not become an excuse for not actually following through and *doing* what is right. Having the right heart and the right attitude is very important, but sometimes people have a good attitude on the inside and it never makes its way to the outside—to their actions and behavior. Part of spiritual maturity is learning to let what's inside of us come out of us.

Things to Think About

1. Why is it important to express through your words and actions what God has placed inside of you?
2. If your heart is right about something, yet you struggle to behave properly, what changes might you make so that your actions will reflect your heart?

CHAPTER 23

Three Keys to a Joy-Filled Life

Colossians 1:28-29

He is the one we proclaim, admonishing and teaching everyone with all wisdom, so that we may present everyone fully mature in Christ. To this end I strenuously contend with all the energy Christ so powerfully works in me.

In today's scripture, Paul declares that Christ is the one he proclaims—not himself, not anyone else, but Christ. He teaches wisely, with one goal in mind: to "present everyone fully mature in Christ." This should be the goal of anyone who teaches and preaches God's Word. At the same time, all believers should desire and seek to become more and more spiritually mature and include spiritual growth among our personal goals.

> Joy is very infectious; therefore, always be full of joy.
> Mother Teresa of Calcutta

There are many ways to grow in Christ, but I would like to focus on just three of them today. All of them relate to the way you spend your time: time with God, time in God's Word, and time with people who will help you grow.

1. Time with God

There is nothing better than one-on-one time with God. During this time, you can read, study, pray, and talk with God, or simply sit in His presence and rest in Him. I once heard that people can be as close to God as they want to be; it all depends on how much time they are willing to put into their personal relationship with Him. Spending time with God is not a religious obligation; it is a wonderful privilege.

2. Time in God's Word

I encourage you to devote as much time as possible to studying and meditating on God's Word. Investing time in God's Word as part of your everyday life is one of the best actions you can take to grow spiritually. In fact, it's an absolute necessity. The Word will guide you, encourage you, give you wisdom, and give you the confidence you need to face each day. Spending time in God's Word does not always mean reading the Bible. You can also read books that help explain the Bible or offer teachings on a particular subject about which you are interested in learning more. You can also listen to podcasts, watch good sermons on television, or learn from various kinds of social media outlets.

3. Time with people who will help you grow

If you really want to grow spiritually, it is vital to spend time with people who can help you, people who are also hungry for the things of God. Make a priority of being around people who will build you up in your faith, not people who will try to pull you away from it. Think and pray about the types of people you need in your life as you walk with God, and ask Him to bring them across your path and help you build godly relationships with them.

If you have friends who are tearing you down and bringing too much temptation into your life, you may find it necessary to separate from them for your own good.

You always have the option to spend your time or to invest it. I can think of no greater way to use your time than to invest it in ways that will help you grow spiritually. You are investing time by reading this book, and I believe it will help and strengthen you not just right now, but for weeks and months to come. The lessons and principles you are learning today will come back to you just when you need them in the future.

Things to Think About

1. Which personal goal would you like to pursue for greater spiritual growth—time with God, time in God's Word, or time with people who encourage you to grow? Make a plan to help you grow in that area.

2. In addition to time with God, time in God's Word, and time with people who will help you grow, what are some other ways you can invest in your spiritual maturity?

CHAPTER 24

Make the Most of Every Opportunity

2 Corinthians 5:20 AMPC

So we are Christ's ambassadors, God making His appeal as it were through us. We [as Christ's personal representatives] beg you for His sake to lay hold of the divine favor [now offered you] and be reconciled to God.

Today's scripture grips my heart every time I read it. Just think about it for a moment: You and I are personal representatives of Christ and should behave as He would in every situation. Jesus came that we might have and enjoy our lives (John 10:10), and when people see us doing that, it makes them want to know how they can have it also.

Have you ever thought about the fact that you may be the only representative of Jesus that the people around you will ever see? This is true, so it's no wonder Paul urges us to be wise in our interactions with others. Here are three simple suggestions to consider when dealing with people, especially those who do not know Christ.

1. Help people feel good about themselves.

You can always start with a smile. A smile can brighten up a moment and help people feel at ease very quickly. You can also say something that will help people feel positive about themselves, even if it's a simple compliment about what they are wearing or the way they style their hair. They may not remember the exact words you spoke, but they will remember that you made them feel good.

> *If you have no joy, there's a leak in your Christianity somewhere.*
>
> Billy Sunday

2. Be peaceful and stay stable.

In our world today, negative emotions are visible everywhere. Whether it's a child throwing a tantrum in a grocery store, a teenager sobbing while talking to a friend in a coffee shop, or someone with road rage, the level of emotional intensity is high. I am sure that many people who seem angry and offended would like to have peace, but they have no idea how to get it.

If you can be the stable person when others are stressed or anxious in your workplace, your neighborhood, your family, or any other group, people will notice. They will pay attention when you can stay calm while everyone is upset, and it won't be long before they start asking you why. Once they open the door by asking about why you are so peaceful, you can simply tell them it is because you have Jesus in your life helping you at all times and that He is available to them also.

If they accept what you say, share as much as they are willing to hear. If they reject what you say, simply continue to demonstrate the fruit of the Holy Spirit and pray for them.

Circumstances are not to be in control of your emotions. With God's help, you can remain emotionally steady when everyone else is tossed about emotionally by circumstances.

3. Value people.

Many people today do not feel special, loved, or valued at all. As Christians, we know the opposite is true.

Everyone is precious to God, and demonstrating that we value them is one of the best gifts we can give them.

There are many simple ways to show people they are important: express interest in the things that interest them, take time to listen and be compassionate when they need to talk about a problem, meet a practical need in their lives, sit with them at lunch, ask how they are doing during a break at work, or show support if they are going through a difficult time. Helping people feel valued does not require a lot of time, money, or effort, but it makes a significant impact.

In addition, I would encourage you to pray and regularly ask God to give you wisdom when dealing with unbelievers and to help you make the most of every opportunity you have with them. He dearly loves each one, and you never know when He might use you to make an eternal difference in their lives.

Things to Think About

1. In what practical ways can you be a good ambassador for Christ to the people around you, especially those who do not know Him?
2. How can you help someone feel valued and special? Who is it?

CHAPTER 25

Christ in You, Part 1

Colossians 1:27

To them God has chosen to make known among the Gentiles the glorious riches of this mystery, which is Christ in you, the hope of glory.

Today and tomorrow, we will focus on Colossians 1:27, which is one of the most powerful and amazing verses in the New Testament. Understanding this verse and living in its truth is essential to a life of joy and strength, but sometimes we read it quickly, without stopping to consider what it really means. The word *glory* means the manifestation of all the excellence of God. We cannot be glorified without Christ living in us, helping us every moment to be what He desires. On the other hand, we are His only hope of glory here on earth because He works through us. One way He shows His power and greatness is in the fact that He changes people—heals us, sets us free, makes us emotionally strong and stable, and gives us a sense of meaning and purpose, among other things—after we receive Him as Savior and Lord.

Christ in us is "the hope of glory," but what does it mean for Him to be "in" us? Jesus came to live in your heart through the Holy Spirit when you believed in and received Him. This means that you are His home. You are never left alone. You never have to do anything alone. You are never far away from the help or the hope you need. God is never more than one thought away from you. The moment you turn your thoughts toward Him, you become aware of how near He is to you.

> *The fullness of joy is to behold God in everything.*
> Julian of Norwich

Let me use a biological example to explain this further. When a man and a woman have a sexual relationship and the husband's seed is planted in his wife's womb, she becomes pregnant with his child. When Christ comes to live in a believer's heart, we become pregnant, so to speak, with everything God is. Jesus is called the "Seed" (Genesis 3:15 NKJV); He is the seed of everything God is and has done in us (Galatians 3:16, 19; John 3:9).

You may be pregnant with all kinds of spiritual truths, so to speak, but you have not given birth to them yet. You may even be feeling the birth pains of labor. Paul writes to his spiritual children, "I am again in the pains of childbirth until Christ is formed in you" (Galatians 4:19). Paul deeply desired for the believers to be fully formed into the image of Christ. He wanted to present them spiritually mature. We want that also, and like Paul, sometimes we feel the pangs of labor as we allow God to bring forth something new in our lives.

When a woman is pregnant, she believes she will hold her baby in her arms when she delivers. The baby is alive in her, but it has not yet come forth into the world where she can see it, hear it, hold it, and talk to it. She knows she will have to endure a time of waiting and preparation before she has her baby, but knowing that her child is coming into the world gives her immeasurable joy. The same principle applies to your life spiritually. Seeds have been planted in you as a believer—seeds of goodness, seeds of love, seeds of peace, seeds of joy, seeds of righteousness, and others—but they will not burst into a harvest overnight. In time, as you continue to walk with God in obedience to Him and as you grow in your knowledge of Him, the seeds will develop into good fruit in your behavior that will please God and draw others to Him.

Things to Think About

1. In your own words, describe why Christ in you is "the hope of glory."
2. What are some good seeds God has placed in you?

CHAPTER 26

Christ in You, Part 2

Colossians 1:27

To them God has chosen to make known among the Gentiles the glorious riches of this mystery, which is Christ in you, the hope of glory.

Today we look again at Colossians 1:27, a verse that will change your life as you understand it and live by it. Yesterday I explained that God places many good things inside of us when we receive Jesus as Lord and Savior and that these good things take time to fully develop. This means that you already have everything you need inside of you. You simply need to believe it.

> *A joyless life is not a Christian life, for joy is one constant recipe for Christian living.*
> William Barclay

The enemy does everything he can to cause you *not* to believe God has given you everything you need and *not* to realize who you are in Christ. Even though you have been made new in Christ, he will use your old desires and habits to tempt you to grow discouraged spiritually. He wants you to forget that you are a new creation in Christ (2 Corinthians 5:17) and that Christ now lives in you by the Holy Spirit (2 Timothy 1:14). He will tempt you to act in ungodly ways, but you don't have to wear yourself out fighting bad behavior. This can feel like a spiritual battle—and it is. All you need to do in order to win this battle is remember who you are in Christ and remind yourself that He lives in you and has made you new. Continue studying God's Word and spend time with Him. When you are deeply rooted in God's love and you know who you are in Christ, exercising self-control and making good choices instead of yielding to the enemy's temptation is not difficult. If you are steadfast and diligent, you will see continuous good changes in yourself.

Trying to live a life that honors God in your own strength, without abiding in Christ, will only frustrate you. So decide instead to receive the grace God extended to you and let Him do the work of changing you into the person He has given you the ability to be. No amount of human effort to change yourself will be effective unless you go to God and say, "I really want to live better, but nothing I try will work without You. I know You have put good things in me, but I need You to bring them out of me. Help me, Lord, to give birth to what You have already placed in me."

The process of manifesting who we are in Christ does not come quickly or without opposition because the devil continues to lie to us. It is important to remember that anything that does not agree with God's Word is a lie, and until we stop believing lies, we won't see the changes we desire.

I have learned many lessons about walking with God, and I am still learning. I am also still uncovering lies the devil has used to deceive me. If you find yourself frustrated along your journey of spiritual growth, just remember not to turn against yourself—not to live feeling guilty, ashamed, or condemned, wondering what is wrong with you because you can't do everything right. We all make mistakes. You do not have to compare your spiritual growth to anyone else's. All you need to do is to believe the Word of God, stay in fellowship with Jesus, and keep on keeping on. The more you keep going forward in Christ and refuse to quit, the more spiritually strong and stable you will become. Every day you don't quit is a day you make progress.

Things to Think About

1. The next time the enemy tries to get you to believe a lie about who you are in Christ or about your relationship with God, how will you respond?
2. In what ways have you been trying to change yourself? How can you allow the Holy Spirit to change you instead?

CHAPTER 27

The Joy of Walking in Love

Galatians 5:13-14

You, my brothers and sisters, were called to be free. But do not use your freedom to indulge the flesh; rather, serve one another humbly in love. For the entire law is fulfilled in keeping this one command: "Love your neighbor as yourself."

Other than the importance of receiving salvation through faith in Christ, I believe learning to walk in love is the most important lesson in God's Word. Jesus says that love is the most important commandment (Mark 12:28–31). Paul writes that love is the greatest thing (1 Corinthians 13:13), and he tells Timothy that the purpose of their teaching is "love, which comes from a pure heart and a good conscience and a sincere faith" (1 Timothy 1:5).

If I were only allowed to teach three messages for the remainder of my life, the first would be that we are saved by grace through our faith in Jesus, and by it we are justified and made right with God. The second would be the importance of spending regular quality time with God. And the third would be receiving God's love, loving Him in return, and walking in love with other people. Thankfully, I don't have to limit my teaching to three subjects, but I share this only to show you how important I believe walking in love is. After we are saved by grace, if we were to focus solely on loving other people, we would have more joy in our lives and avoid most of our problems.

> May Christ be our joy, our confidence, our all. May we daily be made more like to Him, and more devoted to His service.
> Matthew Henry, *Complete Commentary* (Matthew 22:41–46)

Love does no harm to anyone. People who walk in love

cannot be unhappy, because they don't have their minds on themselves but on what they can do for God and others. I have often said that we cannot be both selfish and happy at the same time, and love is the polar opposite of selfishness.

The love I am referring to is not a carnal (human) love. It is not a feeling, although it may include feelings. It is the same kind of love God gives to us. It is unconditional, everlasting, and powerful. It is called the "royal law" of liberty (James 2:8) because the person who loves will not break any of the commandments. If we love God as we should, we will happily obey Him, and one of His commands is that we should love one another. In fact, Jesus says, "A new command I give you: Love one another. As I have loved you, so you must love one another. By this everyone will know that you are my disciples, if you love one another" (John 13:34–35).

Love is something that can be seen and felt, and it is displayed in a variety of ways. First Corinthians 13 is often called the "love chapter" of the Bible, and in verses 4–8, Paul offers this description of love:

> Love is patient, love is kind. It does not envy, it does not boast, it is not proud. It does not dishonor others, it is not self-seeking, it is not easily angered, it keeps no record of wrongs. Love does not delight in evil but rejoices with the truth. It always protects, always trusts, always hopes, always perseveres. Love never fails.

When I teach about love, I offer this summary of 1 Corinthians 13:4–8: Love is patient with people, and it always believes the best about them. Love helps others, it gives, and it is quick to forgive. This is a very basic list, but these five qualities of love alone are plenty to think about and ask God to help us do.

I highly recommend that we all focus on walking in love. This requires intentionality and saying no to self regularly. It may seem difficult to do, but when we love someone, we want to sacrifice for them and we find joy in expressing our love for them in this way.

Things to Think About

1. How can you experience joy by serving someone through love today?
2. What kind of sacrifice will you make for someone this week, simply to show them that you love them?

CHAPTER 28

Avoiding Arguments Increases Joy

2 Timothy 2:23-24

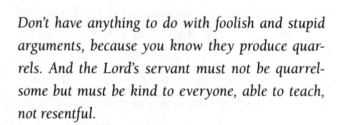

Don't have anything to do with foolish and stupid arguments, because you know they produce quarrels. And the Lord's servant must not be quarrelsome but must be kind to everyone, able to teach, not resentful.

When you think of the way you feel during an argument, what words come to mind? I'm sure that *joyful* is not one of them. Arguments and quarrels with other people quench the joy in our hearts and leave us feeling angry, upset, rejected, frustrated, confused, or sad. This is why Paul urges us in today's Scripture passage to diligently avoid foolish talk, arguments, or quarrels. In the New King James Version, this reads: "But avoid foolish and ignorant disputes, knowing that they generate strife."

Paul also notes that those who serve the Lord "must be kind to everyone." The Amplified Bible, Classic Edition renders this as "must be kindly to everyone and mild-tempered [preserving the bond of peace]." I like to summarize this by saying that God's people should be makers and maintainers of peace, which means we should be diligent not to engage in strife.

We don't hear the word *strife* often, but it is characterized by unpleasantness in relationships, contention, bickering, arguing, offense, or heated disagreements. When strife is present, an angry undercurrent flows among individuals or groups of people, causing tension and quarrels. Strife

> *Joy, not grit, is the hallmark of holy obedience. We need to be lighthearted in what we do to avoid taking ourselves too seriously. It is a cheerful revolt against self and pride.*
>
> Richard J. Foster,
> *Freedom of Simplicity*

destroys marriages, families, friendships, businesses, and churches. It is a tool Satan uses to stop the will of God. Strife is a fruit of pride (Proverbs 13:10). Strife is dangerous and destructive, like a deadly, contagious disease, and it spreads rapidly unless people confront it.

It is important for us as people of God to avoid foolish arguments and strife and to be willing to humble ourselves and do all we can do to maintain peace with others. Paul knew the power believers have when we live in unity and agreement (Matthew 18:19), and he told the Philippians they would complete his joy if they lived in harmony (Philippians 2:2 AMPC). We must pursue peace, crave it, and seek it with all of our hearts (Psalm 34:14 AMPC). Without peace, we are without power and without joy.

I urge you not to get involved in conversations that lead to strife. Avoid controversies over issues that do not even matter, and refuse to be involved in gossip and tale-bearing, which are ungodly and unnecessary. Do not spread rumors or tell other people's secrets. These things cause angry undercurrents, spark resentment, undermine trust, and hinder God's power. Many homes cannot prosper and be blessed because everyone is in strife. Mom and Dad bicker and argue; the siblings argue and resent one another. The entire family forfeits the joy and blessing God intends for them, and no one is happy except the enemy.

I want to repeat that strife is very dangerous and that, as people who serve God, we must do everything we can do to avoid it. According to Psalm 133, when people dwell in unity, life is good and pleasant. Unity releases anointing

(God's presence and power), and it is also where God commands His blessing to be released.

When Dave and I began Joyce Meyer Ministries, God clearly instructed us to stay out of strife. He showed us that He could not bless us and we would not succeed if we allowed strife in our marriage, our home, or our ministry. We have worked diligently over the years to keep strife out of our lives. This requires willingness to constantly communicate and confront issues.

Some people think strife will go away if they simply ignore it, but this is not true; it must be dealt with. I encourage you to ask the Holy Spirit to help you be a person who avoids strife, restores peace, and spreads joy everywhere you go.

Things to Think About

1. In what ways can you bring peace to overcome the strife you may be dealing with in any of your relationships?
2. How would the absence of strife in your life increase your joy?

CHAPTER 29

Put Old Ways behind You

Colossians 3:5-11

Put to death, therefore, whatever belongs to your earthly nature: sexual immorality, impurity, lust, evil desires and greed, which is idolatry. Because of these, the wrath of God is coming. You used to walk in these ways, in the life you once lived. But now you must also rid yourselves of all such things as these: anger, rage, malice, slander, and filthy language from your lips. Do not lie to each other, since you have taken off your old self with its practices and have put on the new self, which is being renewed in knowledge in the image of its Creator. Here there is no Gentile or Jew, circumcised or uncircumcised, barbarian, Scythian, slave or free, but Christ is all, and is in all.

As you read today's Scripture passage, you can see that there is nothing joyful about the negative behaviors it mentions. Because the habits on this list are so detrimental, Paul says to put them "to death." In spiritual terms, this means to choose to crucify the flesh and die to self with the help of the Holy Spirit. All believers are called to do this. Paul writes that he personally knows what this means: "May I never boast except in the cross of our Lord Jesus Christ, through which the world has been crucified to me, and I to the world" (Galatians 6:14). And in Galatians 2:20 he says, "I have been crucified with Christ and I no longer live, but Christ lives in me." Spiritually speaking, this happened when Christ died and rose from the dead. Now, we are in the process of learning how to walk in what He purchased for us with His blood.

> *Rejoice in the Lord and be glad, you righteous; sing, all you who are upright in heart!*
>
> Psalm 32:11

When new believers read these verses, they may think, *Imagine putting to death all those negative things! That must be so wonderful!* Later, they think, *I'm just not there yet. I don't even think I'm close!* They don't always realize that Paul had followed Christ for twenty years by the time he wrote these words. This should give everyone hope. The question is not whether we have "arrived"; it is *Are we growing?*

We don't please God by doing everything perfectly all

the time. We please God by having faith, loving Him, and wanting to mature in Him. Remember always that a person with a right heart who makes some mistakes is much better positioned for spiritual growth than someone with perfect behavior but an impure heart.

Paul does use strong language in Colossians 3:5–11 when he says, "Put to death..." He is not encouraging violence against yourself; he is trying to make the point that sin must be dealt with firmly and decisively. When you know you have sin in your life, the first important thing to do is repent of it and begin praying regularly that God will strengthen you and enable you to stand against temptation. If a specific person tempts you to sin, you may have to adjust or discontinue that friendship. If your job requires you to do things that you know are wrong, you will have to get another job. If you are overweight and candy is a big temptation to you, then don't buy it. When God shows you an action to take, it is important to obey Him. Obedience to God means adjusting or eliminating anything in our lives that is not in harmony with Him. The more we live in harmony with Him, the more our peace and joy increase.

The best way I know to crucify the flesh in your practical, everyday life is simply not to feed it. You can kill anything if you starve it. Every time we give in to an ungodly whim or desire, we feed the enemy. But each time we resist those temptations, the fleshly trait becomes weaker and weaker until it eventually dies. As we deny the flesh and feed the things of God by doing what His Word teaches us to do, we grow spiritually and enjoy His blessings.

Let me encourage you today to think about what steals your joy. Decide that you will not feed it anymore and that, instead, you will focus on thoughts and actions that will increase the joy that God has given you.

Things to Think About

1. What do you need to "put to death" (eliminate) in your life in order for your joy to increase?
2. Why does having a pure heart toward God—even though your behavior may be imperfect—position you to grow spiritually?

CHAPTER 30

Follow the Umpire of Your Soul

Colossians 3:15 AMPC

And let the peace (soul harmony which comes) from Christ rule (act as umpire continually) in your hearts [deciding and settling with finality all questions that arise in your minds, in that peaceful state] to which as [members of Christ's] one body you were also called [to live]. And be thankful (appreciative), [giving praise to God always].

Peace is important for many reasons, but one of them is that it leads to joy. When we have peace, we can have joy, and when we have joy we can have peace. I like the way the Amplified Bible, Classic Edition renders today's verse, because the idea of peace as an umpire in our hearts helps us understand how God uses His gift of peace to help us in our lives.

In a baseball game, the umpire has the final say regarding whether a player is safe or out. If the player is safe, he can continue playing. If he is out, he must leave the game temporarily. Peace is similar to an umpire in that it lets us know what we should allow in our lives and what we should eliminate. First Corinthians 14:33 tells us that "God is not a God of disorder but of peace," and Ephesians 2:14 says that Jesus "himself is our peace." When God gives us peace about something, we know it is right for us, and when He doesn't give us peace, we know it is wrong for us.

> When we are told to rejoice evermore, *it follows immediately,* Pray without ceasing. *See how high we are to aim in prayer—not only at peace, but joy.*
> Matthew Henry, *Complete Commentary* (John 15:11)

We need to learn to follow peace when we make decisions. Many people make decisions based on what they *want* to do or what they *think* seems good. Human thoughts and desires can be very strong, so it is extremely important that we submit our desires to the leading of the Holy Spirit. Only He knows what is best for us.

It is possible for us to become so excited about something that we talk ourselves into doing it and push to make it happen, even if we really don't have peace about it. Psalm 127:1 says, "Unless the Lord builds the house, the builders labor in vain." It doesn't say the builders cannot build it, but that their hard work is fruitless.

When we feel very excited about something, our enthusiasm can override any lack of peace we may sense deep in our hearts. I have learned that when I am unusually excited about something, the best course of action for me is not to act right away. It's smarter for me to wait a little while, let the enthusiasm settle down, and then see what I think about the situation. Sometimes I feel peace and move ahead; sometimes I don't. But at least I give myself a chance to see if peace is there or not.

If you have ever paid the price for moving forward with a decision when you did not have peace about it, you know what I mean. It could be something as simple as buying something you really, really wanted, even though a feeling inside you said not to do it. Or it could be something as complicated as getting deeply involved in a relationship that affected several people when you knew in your heart it was not right. When we fail to follow peace and have to live with the consequences of that decision, it helps us learn how to be led by peace in the future.

I want to add that peace is one of the primary ways we hear from God. God leads and reveals His will to us in many different ways. When He is truly leading us, we have a deep sense of peace in our hearts about the direction in which He wants us to go. Our flesh may not like everything about it, but the peace in our hearts, or the lack of it, will tell us what is right.

Things to Think About

1. If you have ever felt a lack of peace about something but moved forward anyway, what lessons did that experience teach you?
2. When you have allowed peace to be the umpire of your soul, how did your joy increase as you followed that peace?

CHAPTER 31

New Life in Christ

Ephesians 2:1-2, 4-7 **NKJV**

And you He made alive, who were dead in trespasses and sins, in which you once walked according to the course of this world...But God, who is rich in mercy, because of His great love with which He loved us, even when we were dead in trespasses, made us alive together with Christ (by grace you have been saved), and raised us up together, and made us sit together in the heavenly places in Christ Jesus, that in the ages to come He might show the exceeding riches of His grace in His kindness toward us in Christ Jesus.

Before you and I came alive in Christ, we were spiritually dead and separated from God because of sin. We walked in sin and lived according to the world's ways, unknowingly following the ways of Satan, the enemy of God's purpose and will. We may have been completely unaware of our sin because we were dead to God, meaning that we had no relationship with Him and were not in any way led by His Spirit. If you remember your life before you accepted Jesus as your Savior, you probably remember that it was devoid of peace and joy.

But God intervened for all of us, and even when we were not interested in Him at all, He cared about us. Through Christ, He made a way for us to be delivered from the bondage of sin and the misery of separation from Him. Jesus paid the price for us to become spiritually alive in Him, to be completely forgiven of our sin and given a new life. He did this because He loves us. In today's verses, Paul reminds the Ephesians of what an amazing gift this new life is. All we need to do is believe and surrender our lives to Him.

> *The life God has provided for us through Jesus Christ is a precious gift, and we should enjoy every moment of it.*
> Joyce Meyer, *The Confident Woman Devotional*

Paul uses only two short words to open Ephesians 2:4, but they are powerful: "But God." This means that God provided an answer to the dilemma in which people live without Christ. "But God" is the transition from hopelessness to hope and from complete negativity to positivity. The people were dead in sin, but God intervened. Spiritually speaking, He raised them up and seated them in heavenly places because they were in Christ. This is still true for everyone who believes.

The phrase "but God" is used often in Scripture. In many instances, it is in connection with God's delivering power (1 Samuel 23:14; Psalm 49:15; Psalm 73:26; Romans 5:8). Notice that the apostle John writes that the devil comes to kill, steal, and destroy, *but* Jesus Christ came to earth that we might "have and enjoy life, and have it in abundance [to the full, till it overflows]" (John 10:10 AMP). No matter how much Satan seeks our harm and destruction, God always has a plan for our rescue and victory. No matter what we go through, God is always aware of it and always able to intervene.

God not only raised us up when we were dead in sin, but He gave us the very life of Christ and seated us in heavenly places (Ephesians 2:5–6). I don't want you to miss the power of this truth, so let me explain what it means: When Jesus had accomplished all that His Father sent Him to earth to do, the Father raised Jesus up and seated Him at His own right hand, to wait for His enemies to become a stool for His feet (Hebrews 10:12–13). In other words, Jesus is now at perfect rest and peace, and if we are seated with Him, then that same rest and peace is available to us.

The next time you begin to feel upset about something

in your life, tell your emotions to take their seat in Christ and trust Him to do what you cannot do. Your life before Christ may have been characterized by worry, fear, and anxiety, but now that you are in Him, you can have a life of rest, peace, and joy.

Things to Think About

1. Can you think of a "but God" moment in your life—a situation in which you were headed in one direction and God intervened to turn things around? Remember that and thank Him for it today.

2. When you think about the new life God has given you in Christ, how does it enable you to find rest, peace, and joy?

CHAPTER 32

Keep Doing Good

Galatians 6:9-10

Let us not become weary in doing good, for at the proper time we will reap a harvest if we do not give up. Therefore, as we have opportunity, let us do good to all people, especially to those who belong to the family of believers.

When we do what is right and good over a period of time, and we believe we are sowing good seed but not reaping a good harvest, we can become frustrated. But Paul urges us to not grow weary of doing good or doing what is right. We should not do what is right simply to receive a reward, but we should do it because it is right. Sometimes this means having to treat someone well for a long time before they begin to treat us well in return. Perhaps they will never treat us well, but our reward comes from God, not from other human beings. When we look to people for accolades, appreciation, or blessings, we may be very disappointed, but when we look to God, He never forgets what we have done, and He knows exactly how to bless us.

> Joy must be one of the pivots of our life. It is the token of a generous personality.
> Mother Teresa of Calcutta

I firmly believe that anyone who follows God's principles consistently will end up enjoying a good life. Those who come to God must "believe that he exists and that he rewards those who earnestly seek him" (Hebrews 11:6). God's promises never fail. Their fulfillment may take longer than we would like, but if we don't grow weary and we keep doing what is right, our reward will come.

After his encouragement not to become weary of doing good in Galatians 6:9, Paul goes on to offer an instruction that has changed my life. Those who study God's Word usually have certain scriptures that impact their lives in a major way, and Galatians 6:10 is one of those for me. Paul writes: "As we have opportunity, let us do good to all people, especially to those who belong to the family of believers." In the Amplified Bible, Classic Edition, this verse reads, "Be mindful to be a blessing, especially to those of the household of faith." To be mindful means to have your mind full of something, or to purposefully think about it. We might say that in this verse, it means to think deliberately about how we can bless others.

During a period of time when I was seeking to know what loving other people meant in practical terms, this verse gave me a simple instruction. And as I have followed it, my joy has increased. I have formed the habit of taking time to think intentionally of ways I can bless other people. I encourage you to ask God to show you how you can bless specific people in your life, and I believe He will. Learn to listen to people, because they usually tell you in the course of conversation what they need, like, or want. If you are able, then try to make that happen for them. The less we have our minds on ourselves, the happier we become.

You might hear a friend mention that their weekend babysitter canceled and that they will have to miss something they were really looking forward to because they could not find a substitute. Perhaps you know someone you could suggest to babysit, or maybe you could keep the children yourself. You might overhear a single mom say that she hasn't been able to take her family out to eat in months, and you could give her a gift certificate to a restaurant. I could make many suggestions, but I'm sure you get the point. Don't let opportunities to help others pass you by without at least giving some creative thought to ways you might help them. It will be life changing. Do good intentionally, and don't grow weary of doing it!

Things to Think About

1. Have you grown weary in doing good? How does today's reading encourage you to keep doing what is right and good?
2. Have you recently heard anyone mention something they might need? How can you meet this need?

CHAPTER 33

Finding Joy in the Midst of Suffering

Colossians 1:24

Now I rejoice in what I am suffering for you, and I fill up in my flesh what is still lacking in regard to Christ's afflictions, for the sake of his body, which is the church.

Perhaps more than any other biblical writer, Paul knew how to rejoice in suffering. He writes about his difficult experiences in 2 Corinthians 11:23–27:

> I have...been exposed to death again and again. Five times I received from the Jews the forty lashes minus one. Three times I was beaten with rods, once I was pelted with stones, three times I was shipwrecked...I have been in danger from rivers, in danger from bandits, in danger from my fellow Jews, in danger from Gentiles; in danger in the city, in danger in the country, in danger at sea; and in danger from false believers. I have labored and toiled and have often gone without sleep; I have known hunger and thirst and have often gone without food; I have been cold and naked.

Happiness is caused by things that happen around me, and circumstances will mar it; but joy flows right on through trouble; joy flows on through the dark; joy flows in the night as well as in the day; joy flows through all persecution and opposition.

Dwight L. Moody

Obviously, Paul was well acquainted with suffering. In addition to the hardships he mentions in today's passage, he was also jailed on multiple occasions and spent several years in prison. He learned to rejoice in his suffering, so he knows exactly what he is asking of us when he urges us to rejoice in ours.

We don't rejoice *because* we are suffering. No one enjoys suffering, but we can rejoice that we have hope through Christ in the midst of our pain and struggles. This reminds me of 1 Thessalonians 5:18, where Paul instructs us to "give thanks *in* all circumstances" (emphasis mine). He doesn't say to give thanks *for* all circumstances, but he knows that no matter what happens, we can give thanks in the midst of difficult situations because we have a relationship with God and He is always with us. Paul explains the value of rejoicing in difficult seasons in Romans 5:3–4: "We also glory in our sufferings, because we know that suffering produces perseverance; perseverance, character; and character, hope."

The apostle James also writes about the positive aspects of suffering as believers in Christ: "Consider it *pure joy*, my brothers and sisters, whenever you face trials of many kinds, because you know that the testing of your faith produces perseverance" (James 1:2–3, emphasis mine). Most people do not immediately respond to trials with joy. We may be tempted to complain, to become angry, to get depressed, or to grow fearful. Those would be natural and understandable reactions, but Christians can respond differently because we know that God is on our side, and that He is our Deliverer, Vindicator, Healer—and everything else we need.

James says to rejoice in trials because they produce perseverance. But they can produce a lot of negative emotions before perseverance shows itself strongly. If we let it happen, trials can pull us into self-pity, pride, fear, rebellion, selfishness, jealousy, or other harmful conditions. We don't need to allow negativity to control how we view the difficult seasons of our lives.

Paul sets a wonderful example of rejoicing in the midst of trials and pain, and James says to consider our suffering "pure joy." Both of these apostles affirm that suffering produces perseverance. It makes us strong in the Lord. I have suffered some painful situations in my life, and I do not take suffering lightly. I realize that rejoicing in the midst of trials is not easy, but I encourage you to do it. We don't have to be happy about suffering, but we can choose to endure it with the joy of the Lord in our hearts. As we do, He will strengthen us and release more and more grace to carry us through it.

Things to Think About

1. How has God used suffering to strengthen you and draw you closer to Him?
2. Think about something that has caused you to suffer. How could you have found joy in the midst of those circumstances? Remember this next time you go through a difficult season.

CHAPTER 34

Don't Be Anxious about Anything

Philippians 4:6-7

Do not be anxious about anything, but in every situation, by prayer and petition, with thanksgiving, present your requests to God. And the peace of God, which transcends all understanding, will guard your hearts and your minds in Christ Jesus.

Today's Scripture passage offers us four practical and powerful principles: Don't worry. Pray. Be thankful. Enjoy peace. I can't tell you how often I meditate on or declare these verses, especially when the enemy tempts me to worry.

Most of us have many opportunities to worry and be anxious, but we can choose to handle things differently. Instead of worrying, we can pray about what we need or want. We can pray about the situations that concern us, and through prayer we can invite God to work in those circumstances. While we are presenting our petitions to God, we are to live a life of thanksgiving. No matter how many problems we might have, we all have more blessings than difficulties. If we are ungrateful for what we already have, why should God give us more? Wouldn't we merely have more to complain about? We may think we would be happy and grateful if only we didn't have just one certain problem. But experience tells us that unless we have thankful hearts that always look for reasons to be grateful, we will always find something to complain about, no matter what God does for us.

> Joy and laughter are the gifts of living in the presence of God and trusting that tomorrow is not worth worrying about.
>
> Henri Nouwen

Paul assures us that if we refuse to be anxious, that if we

pray and give thanks, God's peace will guard our hearts in a way that "transcends all understanding." Being content or discontent has little to do with our circumstances and everything to do with our heart toward God.

One practical way to avoid worry is to replace "worry thoughts" with thoughts about times you have had problems and God has helped you. Godly thoughts will strengthen your faith. Another way to get your mind off your problem is not to think about it or talk about it continually. Go do something. Get involved in helping someone else who is hurting. Have lunch or coffee with a friend. If you are occupied with something other than your problem, it won't live in the forefront of your mind.

Worry seems almost epidemic in society today. Some people even believe it is their duty to worry about their children when they are out with their friends, but praying for God to grant them wisdom and protect them would be a much better use of their time. I was once a chief worrier, and it took me quite a while to have a breakthrough in this area. I worried until I finally realized that I just simply wasn't intelligent enough to solve my own problems and that I needed God's help. The way to get God's help is through prayer (asking in faith) and living with an attitude of gratitude while you wait for the breakthrough you need.

Worry is useless. It has no positive side effects and many negative ones. It can cause headaches, stress, tension, fear, negative attitudes, stomach problems, sleepless nights, and many other miseries. It is like rocking in a rocking chair, which keeps us busy, but gets us nowhere.

If you have struggled with worry, as I have, let me encourage you that your experience with God's faithfulness will help immensely. Each time God solves a problem for you and you remember it, your faith will gain strength. Consider keeping a gratitude journal in which you record times when God has helped you and brought you victory.

When you are under an attack of worry, instead of striving hard to stop worrying, ask the Holy Spirit to help you; then hold your peace while God works in your situation.

Things to Think About

1. What are the four principles of Philippians 4:6–7? How would applying them to a certain situation in your life help you?
2. Think of a time when God solved a problem for you. How does remembering what He did strengthen your faith?

CHAPTER 35

Choose Thoughts That Lead to Joy, Part 1

Philippians 4:8-9

Finally, brothers and sisters, whatever is true, whatever is noble, whatever is right, whatever is pure, whatever is lovely, whatever is admirable—if anything is excellent or praiseworthy—think about such things. Whatever you have learned or received or heard from me, or seen in me—put it into practice. And the God of peace will be with you.

Today's Scripture passage follows Philippians 4:6–7, which you may remember from yesterday's reading: "Do not be anxious about anything, but in every situation, by prayer and petition, with thanksgiving, present your requests to God. And the peace of God, which transcends all understanding, will guard your hearts and your minds in Christ Jesus." Today, Paul teaches us exactly what to think about while we wait for answers to our prayers and for God's help in dealing with situations that tempt us to be anxious. During these waiting periods, we think about many things. What we think about can either upset us more or help us remain peaceful in the storm. Whatever we think about determines how we will live our lives. Happy thoughts produce a happy life, while negative thoughts cause us to experience life in negative ways. Paul lists seven qualities of things we should think about. Although there are others, these certainly give us a great place to start.

> *When you're tempted to be upset, ask yourself, "Is this worth giving up my joy?"*
> Joel Osteen

1. True

If we think and talk about our circumstances, we may be thinking and talking about the facts in our lives at the current time, but Jesus promises that the truth will set us free (John 8:32). Truth is greater than facts, and it can ultimately change them. We may have a problem to which we don't have an answer and that is the fact, but the truth is that God does know the answer. His truth can alter the facts of any situation, and I have seen this happen many times. He loves us and will never leave us helpless. He is our Deliverer, and He is faithful. Remember, John 8:32 says, "You will know the truth, and the truth will set you free." Keep lifting up the truth of God's Word and let it work against any facts that don't agree with it.

2. Noble

The word *noble* isn't used much in our society today, but it's an important word for us to understand. The Amplified Bible, Classic Edition version of Philippians 4:8 renders "whatever is noble" this way: "whatever is worthy of reverence and is honorable and seemly." A simple definition I like to use for the Greek word for *noble* when it pertains to a person is "having or showing fine personality qualities and high moral character." We can also think of being noble as being an excellent person. Let us think on excellent things—what God has done for us, what we can do for other people in need, ways we can spread the gospel, how we can live a life that glorifies God, and others. There are so many noble and honorable things to meditate on, so why fix our minds on low, base, or negative things? God sets before us death and life, good and evil, and urges us to choose life and good things (Deuteronomy 30:19).

3. Right

To think about what is right means to ponder things that are just and to be fair-minded, unbiased, impartial, and unprejudiced. God is just. He always does what is right, and He is impartial. When we have a situation that is unjust and painful to us, we can trust God to bring justice on our behalf. He takes our ashes and gives us beauty (Isaiah 61:3). God takes bad things and turns them into good things! We should enjoy God's justice in our lives, and we should also strive to be just in our dealings with other people.

The more we think about what is true, noble, and right, according to today's Scripture passage, the more peace and joy we will experience.

Things to Think About

1. Are you waiting for an answer to prayer right now? Are you tempted to be anxious? How can choosing godly thoughts help you in this season?
2. What are some examples of thoughts you can think that are true, noble, and right?

CHAPTER 36

Choose Thoughts That Lead to Joy, Part 2

Philippians 4:8-9

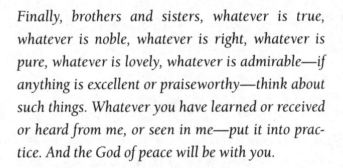

Finally, brothers and sisters, whatever is true, whatever is noble, whatever is right, whatever is pure, whatever is lovely, whatever is admirable—if anything is excellent or praiseworthy—think about such things. Whatever you have learned or received or heard from me, or seen in me—put it into practice. And the God of peace will be with you.

Yesterday we looked at the first part of Philippians 4:8–9, and today we'll look at the last part of this important Scripture passage. I firmly believe that these two verses can change the course of a person's life, because everything we do and say begins with our thoughts. If our thoughts align with God's Word, our lives will also align with His Word—and that is the key to blessing and joy.

> *When we choose to acknowledge God in the midst of our problems, we open the door for Him to begin to work in our situation and for joy to come back to our hearts.*
>
> Joyce Meyer

4. Pure

The Greek word used here for *pure* means "clean." The world today is filled with impurity, and we can be easily tempted to think impure thoughts. Let us have clean thoughts, thoughts that Jesus would think, rather than thoughts the flesh or the world thinks. Jesus says that the pure in heart are blessed, for they shall see God (Matthew 5:8). I believe this refers to the ability of the pure in heart to hear clearly from God and to be more aware of His presence in our daily lives, as well as seeing Him face-to-face when we are taken to our heavenly home.

5. Lovely

The Greek word used in Philippians 4:8 for *lovely* means "pleasing" and "agreeable." Our thoughts should be agreeable with God's Word, and when they are, they will be pleasing to God and will benefit us. One of the best habits we can form as we come into agreement with His Word is to consistently meditate on it. When you meditate on a Bible verse or a spiritual truth, you don't simply read about it and then move on; you consider it thoughtfully and allow it to work itself into your heart and express itself in your life so you will live in agreement with God's Word.

6. Admirable

When we think of people we know, we should think of their strengths and abilities, the qualities we admire about them. We think about the characteristics that make them good examples for others. Everyone has weaknesses we can choose to focus on, but everyone also has strengths upon which we can focus. The decision is up to us, but if we desire joy, we should always focus on good things.

7. Excellent and Praiseworthy

We need to think on matters that are good, excellent, and virtuous. We should think about the best aspects of God and the best things in our lives. We can think of all the good that God does and of the people who are blessings in our lives. We can think positively and fill our thoughts with hope. We can also think of plenty of things that are praiseworthy, which simply means things that give us reasons to praise and thank God. Anything that we can think of that motivates us to give praise and thanks to God is always good to have on our minds!

Let me remind you that our thoughts become our words, and our thoughts and words affect our moods and attitudes. Our thoughts, words, and emotions come together to influence our actions, so we can see that in many ways our thoughts ultimately become our lives. Perhaps we should ask ourselves if we want what we have been thinking about, and if not, make a change for the better.

Things to Think About

1. Take a moment to consider a specific circumstance in your life. How could you think about it in ways that are pure, lovely, admirable, excellent, or praiseworthy?

2. Let me ask you to reread Philippians 4:8–9 in its entirety. How can thinking thoughts that agree with God's Word—such as the ones listed in today's passage—increase the joy in your life?

CHAPTER 37

Nothing Has Value Apart from Christ

Philippians 3:8-9

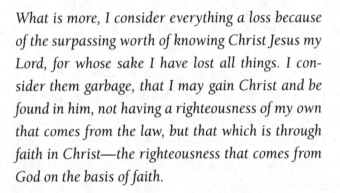

What is more, I consider everything a loss because of the surpassing worth of knowing Christ Jesus my Lord, for whose sake I have lost all things. I consider them garbage, that I may gain Christ and be found in him, not having a righteousness of my own that comes from the law, but that which is through faith in Christ—the righteousness that comes from God on the basis of faith.

Once Paul was enlightened by Christ, he considered everything he had previously thought made him righteous before God to be mere trash (garbage) compared to the privilege of knowing Jesus.

> I delight greatly in the Lord;
> my soul rejoices in my God.
> Isaiah 61:10

The things in which he had formerly placed his hope now seemed worthless. Imagine all the time and effort Paul had put into being well known, admired, self-important, and self-assured. His reputation with people had been more important to him than anything else. His entire worth and value as a man had previously been tied to these attributes and accolades. But when he met Jesus, all of that changed. I think a lot of us can say that once we met Jesus, everything changed.

Paul reached the point where he wanted more than anything to be "in Christ," with no righteousness of his own. This meant that his right standing with God came only by knowing Christ and belonging to Him. Nothing else mattered.

Isaiah tells us that our own righteousness is like filthy rags: "All of us have become like one who is unclean, and all our righteous acts are like filthy rags; we all shrivel up like a leaf, and like the wind our sins sweep us away" (Isaiah 64:6).

Paul never lost his first love for Jesus as so many people do. He passionately pressed on to know Jesus and become

like Him in all of His ways from the day he met Jesus until
the day he died.

I encourage you to follow Paul's example and to be
sure that you stay strong in your faith. Guard against let-
ting what was once a brightly burning fire in your heart
for God to become a pile of barely glowing embers. This
occurs as we begin to seek other things and allow them to
become more important to us than Jesus is. We get busy
with life and find we have no time to seek God through
His Word and prayer on a daily basis. People may have
all the things money can buy, yet lose all that money can
never buy—such as a deep relationship with God through
Christ, the joy of helping others, and good relationships
with family and friends. People who are dying never ask to
see their bank balance; they want God, family, and friends
around them. Sadly, if we spend no time building these
relationships while we are living and healthy, they won't
be available when we want and need them.

We should all take time to examine our lives occasionally and ask ourselves if we are putting our time into
lasting pursuits, or if we are spending too much time on
things that have no true meaning. We can spend our lives
climbing the ladder of success only to find when we reach
the top that our ladder is leaning against the wrong building. We reap according to what we sow (Galatians 6:7);
therefore, if we don't sow time and effort into the right
things, we cannot expect to have right results. Be wise and
do now what you will be happy and satisfied with later.

Upon discovering that we can give up all of our striving

and self-effort and have Christ and His righteousness—instead of trying to earn righteousness ourselves—a burden lifts from us and we can begin to enjoy God and the life He has given us. People often express the amazing joy and peace they have had since receiving this revelation from God.

Things to Think About

1. What has changed in your life since you met Jesus?
2. How can you begin spending more of your time and energy on things that truly matter?

CHAPTER 38

Living by Faith Increases Joy

Romans 1:17 **AMP**

For in the gospel the righteousness of God is revealed, both springing from faith and leading to faith [disclosed in a way that awakens more faith]. As it is written and forever remains written, "The just and upright shall live by faith."

In today's scripture, Paul refers to the words of the Old Testament prophet Habakkuk, who wrote, "The righteous will live by his faith [in the true God]" (Habakkuk 2:4 AMP). The words *righteous, just,* and *upright* are used as synonyms in various translations of this verse. When you read in Scripture about "the righteous," or "the just and upright," you can apply it personally if you have received Jesus as your Lord and Savior.

The just are those who have been justified, or made right with God, by Jesus' death on the cross. To be justified means that God treats us as though we are not sinners and never have been sinners. He treats us as His beloved children. We enter into a relationship of love, confidence, and friendship. We need not fear or worry, because there is no punishment for us. We *live* by our faith that Jesus took our punishment, and we enjoy the victory He won for us.

> *Joy is the serious business of heaven.*
> C. S. Lewis, *Letters to Malcolm*

The word *faith* means belief or absolute trust that something is true, but it also implies loyalty and commitment. Faith begins when we agree that the message of Jesus' death and resurrection is true, and true faith happens when we say, "Not only do I agree that it is true, but I'm willing to stake my life on it."

For some people, the fact that they have faith in Jesus' victory on the cross makes them think they do not need to stand against the wiles of Satan. But the enemy works against all of God's people, and if we are unaware of his operations against us, we will allow him to get away with them. When people don't know they have an enemy and don't stay vigilant against him, they tend to listen to the devil's lies instead of focusing on all that God has done for them.

I once went through an especially difficult time when there was absolutely no joy or peace in my life. Then I read Romans 15:13: "May the God of hope fill you with *all joy and peace* in believing [through the experience of your faith] that by the power of the Holy Spirit you will abound in hope and overflow with confidence in His promises" (AMP, emphasis mine).

That scripture was a key to my breakthrough. I realized exactly what I was doing wrong. I had lost my faith, hope, joy, and peace because I had plunged into doubt and unbelief, allowing the enemy to torment me with his lies. The more he lied to me, the more I struggled to believe God's promises. Romans 15:13 changed my negative thinking and restored my faith as I realized how important believing is. I realized afresh that Jesus loves me so much that He not only forgave my past sins, but He also looked ahead and forgave me for those moments of weakness when I'd fail in the future, those times when I would not live up to all the truth I knew. I renewed my belief in all that God has done for me, and soon my hope, peace, and joy returned.

Then I pondered Paul's words in Romans 1:17, the same scripture I'm writing to you about today: "For in the gospel the righteousness of God is revealed, both springing from faith and leading to faith" (AMP). I learned that I don't have to allow Satan to influence my mind with questions or unbelief. I can live every moment moving from faith to more faith to more faith, and so can you.

Things to Think About

1. Do you truly acknowledge that you are righteous in Christ? Explain.
2. In what ways do you need to renew your faith in all that God has done for you?

CHAPTER 39

Living the Good Life

Titus 2:13–14 **AMPC**

Christ Jesus . . . who gave Himself on our behalf that He might redeem us (purchase our freedom) from all iniquity and purify for Himself a people [to be peculiarly His own, people who are] eager and enthusiastic about [living a life that is good and filled with] beneficial deeds.

In today's scripture, Paul writes that Jesus gave His life so that we could be people who are "eager and enthusiastic" about living a good life and doing things that benefit others. I have written elsewhere in this book about doing good for others, so today, I'd like to focus on the idea of living a good life, a life full of joy and blessings.

Paul makes clear that the reason we can live a good life is that we belong to God because Jesus has redeemed us and purchased our freedom from sin and the enemy. In John 10:10, Jesus speaks of the kind of life He desires for us and contrasts it with the life the devil wants for us. He says, "The thief comes only in order to steal and kill and destroy. I came that they may have and enjoy life, and have it in abundance (to the full, till it overflows)" (AMPC). The enemy is the thief. He wants to steal every good thing God wants to give to us, and to cause us to be apathetic or depressed about all the blessings that are ours to enjoy in Christ.

As God's people, we are not to spend our lives moping around, discouraged, and despondent. We are also not to spend so much time thinking about all of our faults and failures that we lose our hope and enthusiasm about living a good life. We are not to live doubting God's love

> Keep your feet dry, your eyes open, your heart at peace and your soul in the joy of Christ.
>
> Thomas Merton

or questioning all that He has done for us in Christ, but to live in faith, gratitude, and joy because of all the blessings He offers us.

God is not honored when we have bad attitudes toward ourselves. In fact, I believe that thinking or speaking negatively about ourselves is insulting to Him. If you loved and valued a group of people so much that you were willing to suffer horribly and die for them so they could enjoy themselves and their lives, how would you feel if they refused your gift? Hopefully this question communicates the point I am trying to make: God loves us so much that He made the greatest sacrifice imaginable so that we could be free and forgiven and so that we could live in peace and joy. We honor Him when we embrace this gift, but we dishonor Him when we reject it.

Paul knew that he was not perfect, but in Philippians 3:12, he writes that he pressed on "to lay hold of... that for which Christ Jesus (the Messiah) has laid hold" of him and made him His own (AMPC). He was speaking of the quality of life Jesus wanted him to have because he belonged to God. Paul knew he did not deserve such a good life, but for Jesus' sake, he was determined to have it. Likewise, we do not deserve "the good life," but Jesus died to give it to us, so we honor Him when we receive it with eagerness, enthusiasm, and joy.

If you struggle with negative attitudes that hold you back from the good life that God wants you to live, I urge you to make a change today. Choose a new attitude toward yourself, and choose to focus on how much God loves you

and wants to bless you. Decide that you will enjoy everything you do and each day you live. Paul had to make that
choice, I had to make it, and you'll need to make it also if
you want to live in the fullness that is available to you in
Christ.

Things to Think About

1. Why does belonging to God enable you to enjoy a
   good life?
2. Which attitudes do you need to change about yourself in order to enjoy the good life Jesus died to give
   you?

CHAPTER 40

Joy Comes from Relationship

Philippians 3:10-11 **AMPC**

[For my determined purpose is] that I may know Him [that I may progressively become more deeply and intimately acquainted with Him, perceiving and recognizing and understanding the wonders of His Person more strongly and more clearly], and that I may in that same way come to know the power out- flowing from His resurrection [which it exerts over believers], and that I may so share His sufferings as to be continually transformed [in spirit into His likeness even] to His death, [in the hope] that if pos- sible I may attain to the [spiritual and moral] res- urrection [that lifts me] out from among the dead [even while in the body].

Let me ask you today to stop and feel the depth of the cry of Paul's heart in today's Scripture passage. He wasn't satisfied with merely knowing *about* Jesus, or even just knowing Him a little; he wanted to know Him deeply and intimately. That goal, in fact, was his determined purpose, and that's where we find true joy. Many people know about Jesus or believe that He exists, but a much richer quality of life with Him is available to us.

What fuels intimacy with God is giving Him time and including Him in every area of our lives. Spending time with people and seeing them in all kinds of situations is the only way to truly know them. The same principle applies to our relationship with God. It seems that the apostle John had a special, very intimate relationship with Jesus. He referred to himself as the disciple whom Jesus loved (John 13:23; 19:26). That might sound a bit haughty on his part, but it wasn't. John simply loved Jesus and had a real revelation of how much Jesus loved him. His goal, like Paul's, was intimacy with Jesus. I think anyone can be as close to God as they want to be. The level of intimacy a person enjoys with Him depends simply on how much time they are willing to put into building the relationship.

> *Let us seek not the stream, but the fountain; not primarily the joy, but that real and living union with Jesus by which His joy becomes ours.*
>
> Frances Ridley Havergal

The time I am talking about is not an hour spent sitting in a church once a week. It is including God in all we do. He is never more than one thought away from us, so I encourage you to think of Him often, whisper your gratitude to Him for different things all throughout the day, and ask for His help in everything, even in seemingly insignificant things. I ask the Lord to help me before I try to put in my contact lenses, before I work out, or before I approach any project, no matter how small. I am sorry for the times when I have an independent attitude and spend the day doing many tasks without even asking for His help. You might say, "Well, Joyce, you got the things done anyway, so what difference does it make if you didn't ask for God's help?" I may have gotten the things done, but how much more joyfully, more easily, and perhaps more quickly would they have been accomplished with God's help?

I certainly have not perfected this spiritual discipline. Plenty of times, I go about my busy schedule, and when the day is over, I realize I haven't thought of the Lord all day. I'm not suggesting that God will never help us unless we ask for His help in each specific task we undertake, but I believe we honor Him when we do, and doing so is a way to keep Him in our thoughts and stay connected to Him. I am hoping to establish the importance of always realizing how much we need the Holy Spirit's help in all we do. This is not a law we must follow, but a privilege God gives us. It's not an obligation, but a source of peace, joy, and life, so why would we not take advantage of it?

Things to Think About

1. How can you know Jesus more deeply and more intimately?
2. Take a look at your schedule. What can you set aside to make more room for God in your life?

CHAPTER 41

Chosen People Reflecting the Image of Christ

Colossians 3:12-13

Therefore, as God's chosen people, holy and dearly loved, clothe yourselves with compassion, kindness, humility, gentleness and patience. Bear with each other and forgive one another if any of you has a grievance against someone. Forgive as the Lord forgave you.

Colossians 3:12–13 offers us several specific reasons and ways to be joyful, plus some ways to spread joy to others. Let's look at each aspect of today's Scripture passage individually.

> The joy of the hypocrite is but for a moment, but the joy of those who abide in Christ's love is a continual feast.
>
> Matthew Henry, Complete Commentary (John 15:11)

First, Paul says we are "God's chosen people, holy and dearly loved." To be called *holy* or *chosen* is similar to being called consecrated, meaning to be set apart for God's purposes. So Paul appeals here to God's set-apart people, which includes everyone who has received Jesus as Lord and Savior.

Paul also reminds us that God loves us dearly and more than we can imagine. I do not know of any greater cause for joy than the fact that God Himself loves each of us personally and accepts us completely, just the way we are. When we are tempted to doubt God's love, we need look no further than the cross, where He sent His only Son to be punished, to die in our place, and to forgive our sins, making it possible for us to live in a close, personal relationship with Him.

I think about the next portion of this passage in terms of our "spiritual clothing." Leading up to these verses, Paul mentions putting on "the new self" (Colossians 3:10), and Colossians 3:12–13 describes people who manifest the new self. Generally speaking, putting on our spiritual clothing simply means approaching each day with an attitude that says, "God, I don't want any trouble today. I hope everything goes my way, but experience has taught me that this doesn't always happen. If it doesn't, help me to endure whatever comes my way with good temper and without losing the joy that You have given me. And help me to be kind, gentle, and patient toward everyone I meet." These verses encourage us to be like Jesus in our behavior. Jesus never allowed difficulties or unexpected situations to cause Him to lose His peace or His joy, and because His Spirit lives in us, we can follow His example.

The spiritual clothing we can choose to wear includes "compassion, kindness, humility, gentleness and patience." Kindness, gentleness, and patience are mentioned as fruit of the Holy Spirit, along with love, joy, peace, goodness, faithfulness, and self-control (Galatians 5:22–23). Jesus demonstrated kindness, gentleness, and patience, along with humility and compassion, during His ministry. Often in the Gospels, we read that He had compassion for individuals and groups of people and extended kindness to them (Matthew 9:36, 14:14, 20:34; Luke 7:13). Philippians 2:5–8 characterizes His humility, and Paul appealed to the Corinthians "by the humility and gentleness of Christ" (2 Corinthians 10:1). We also read about His patience when Paul writes, "But for that very reason I was shown mercy so that in me, the worst of sinners, Christ Jesus might display his immense patience as an example for those who would believe in him and receive eternal life" (1 Timothy 1:16).

Finally, Paul writes in today's passage that we are to bear with each other and forgive those against whom we hold grievances, reminding us that God has forgiven us. His forgiveness covers all our sin—past, present, and future. Because He has forgiven us, we can choose to forgive others. Forgiveness is not a feeling, but a choice—a choice that leads to freedom and joy. Just as we choose to put on our natural clothing each day, we can choose to put on our spiritual clothing, which includes forgiving others because we have been forgiven.

Things to Think About

1. Which specific aspects of your spiritual clothing do you most need to put on and demonstrate in your everyday life right now?
2. Who do you need to choose to forgive today? Will you make that choice?

CHAPTER 42

A Sign of Spiritual Maturity

Philippians 3:15-16

All of us, then, who are mature should take such a view of things. And if on some point you think differently, that too God will make clear to you. Only let us live up to what we have already attained.

People who live under the weight of guilt and shame rarely experience true joy, because joy is found in freedom, and guilt and shame are forms of bondage. People feel guilty or ashamed for all kinds of reasons, often because they have not learned to forgive themselves (receive God's forgiveness). When Jesus died to forgive us our sins, His sacrifice covered not only the ways we sin against God and other people, but also the things we do to ourselves.

> A joyful heart is good medicine, but a crushed spirit dries up the bones.
>
> Proverbs 17:22 ESV

In today's Scripture passage, Paul makes an important statement that has helped me tremendously as I gained freedom from guilt and shame, and I want to make sure you don't miss the power of it. He says, "All of us, then, who are mature should take such a view of things" (Philippians 3:15). He went on to indicate that if we are missing something we need to see, then God will make it clear to us. In the meantime, we are to live in the truth we have already gained and keep growing.

Why is this so important? Paul is helping us understand that living under guilt once we have repented and received forgiveness is the baby stage of Christianity. Only those who are spiritually mature will believe God's Word more than they believe how they feel or even what they think. Some people think that continually demeaning or berating themselves for their sin is somehow a positive spiritual quality, but that kind of thinking does not agree with Scripture.

I once knew a woman who loved God very much. She had been taught that suffering for her sin was pleasing to God, so she often wore a scratchy patch of wool under her clothing, against her skin, and it was very uncomfortable, of course. The irritating feeling of the wool rubbing her skin, she reasoned, would remind her of how wretched she was. This theology was taught to her in the church she attended and is not at all consistent with God's Word. Jesus suffered and paid for our sins, and He did a complete and perfect job. He does not need us to add anything to it, not even our burden of guilt.

Is guilt anything other than trying to pay for our sins? I think not! Can we pay for our sins by making ourselves miserable and refusing to enjoy life? No! We cannot pay a debt that has already been paid. Think about it: If you had a credit card bill at the end of the month and someone paid the full balance for you, you wouldn't try to pay more, or pay it again, would you? Similarly, trying to pay for our sins when Jesus has already paid for them, I believe, dishonors His sacrifice.

In the verse preceding today's scripture, Paul writes that he *presses on* (Philippians 3:14). I believe we can assume that the devil tried to hold him in the memory of his past mistakes, just as he does us. Thankfully, we can resist the devil and he will flee (James 4:7). Living the victorious Christian life often requires pressing in and pressing on by choosing to move forward beyond guilt, shame, and condemnation. It may require us to face various tests that make us uncomfortable, tests that God permits in our lives to help strengthen us. But, as we keep our gaze straight before us and press toward the prize that God wants for us, we will show ourselves to be "more than conquerors" (Romans 8:37).

Things to Think About

1. How can you begin to believe and live by God's Word more than you believe and live according to your thoughts and feelings?
2. In what specific situation do you need to press on and choose to move beyond guilt and shame?

CHAPTER 43

Delighting in Faith

Colossians 2:1-5

I want you to know how hard I am contending for you and for those at Laodicea, and for all who have not met me personally. My goal is that they may be encouraged in heart and united in love, so that they may have the full riches of complete understanding, in order that they may know the mystery of God, namely, Christ, in whom are hidden all the treasures of wisdom and knowledge. I tell you this so that no one may deceive you by fine-sounding arguments. For though I am absent from you in body, I am present with you in spirit and delight to see how disciplined you are and how firm your faith in Christ is.

Today's Scripture passage conveys Paul's great love and care for believers in the early church and his commitment to their spiritual development. He wrote during a time when false teaching, which he calls "fine-sounding arguments," was rampant in Colossae. This philosophy threatened the church in Colossae and apparently had spread to the nearby city of Laodicea.

Notice the intensity of Paul's emotion in this passage. He says he is "contending" hard for those who would read his letter. In other words, he was fighting fervently for them, praying for them, and endeavoring to teach them all that he could about Christ. He understood the seriousness of the fact that false teachers had sought to cause the early believers to stray from their faith, and he would not let them fall away without making his best effort to keep them close to the truths of Christianity.

> *If we are saved by grace alone, this salvation is a constant source of amazed delight. Nothing is mundane or matter-of-fact about our lives. It is a miracle we are Christians, and the Gospel, which creates bold humility, should give us a far deeper sense of humor and joy. We don't take ourselves too seriously, and we are full of hope for the world.*
> Tim Keller

This was not the first time Paul had dealt with false teaching. Approximately five years before he wrote to the Colossians about this issue, he had written to the Corinthians about it, saying, "But I am afraid that just as Eve was deceived by the serpent's cunning, your minds may somehow be led astray from your sincere and pure devotion to Christ" (2 Corinthians 11:3). Many other translations render this last phrase as the "simplicity" that is in Christ.

Paul knew how dangerous and deceptive false teaching is, and obviously he was deeply grieved by the fact that it was influencing the early believers. In today's passage, Paul encourages his readers in several ways. To paraphrase his instructions, he says for us to keep learning, to continue to walk more and more closely with God, to know who we are in Christ and what belongs to us in Him, and not to be deceived by philosophies or intellectual theories. All of these are important to our spiritual maturity. He clearly states that his goal for his readers is to be "encouraged in heart and united in love," so they could know and understand Christ completely. The better they knew Christ and the more closely they walked with Him, the stronger they could stand against false teaching. The same is true for us today.

Paul spent years ministering and writing so people could fully understand who Jesus is. He wanted them to be hungry to keep learning more and more, just as he was. I cannot think of a more worthy goal for any of us than to have a deep and personal knowledge and understanding of our Lord and Savior, Jesus Christ—not just knowing about Him, but knowing Him. Deception was rampant in Paul's day, but it is even more so in these days, and we need to always be prepared to meet it with the truth of God's Word.

I hope you will pay special attention to the last sentence of today's scripture. Paul says that although he was physically absent from them, "I am present with you in spirit and delight to see how disciplined you are and how firm your faith in Christ is." I mentioned in the introduction to this book that joy can range from extreme hilarity to calm delight. Paul found delight—and joy—in the firm faith of the Colossian believers. You and I can also find joy in our faith. The better we know Christ, the stronger our faith will be, and the greater our joy will be.

Things to Think About

1. What kinds of false teachings are you exposed to in the world today, and how can you stand against them?

2. Why is the statement "The better we know Christ, the stronger our faith will be, and the greater our joy will be" true, and what does it mean to you personally?

CHAPTER 44

Enjoy the Freedom God Has Given You

Romans 6:18

You have been set free from sin and have become slaves to righteousness.

Today's Scripture verse affirms that those of us who are Christians have been set free from sin and from the legalism that causes us to focus excessively on avoiding sin instead of receiving the grace God offers us as His children. The reality of our freedom in Christ should give us great joy.

> God doesn't just want us simply to be alive, but He wants us to enjoy being alive. He wants us to live with joy— abundant, overflowing joy!
>
> Joyce Meyer

As children of God, we should experience the glorious freedom and liberty Jesus died to give us—freedom to enjoy all God has given to us through His Son. But Satan tries to rob us of enjoying our lives. According to John 10:10, he works only to "steal and kill and destroy." He also accuses us, condemns us, and strives to make us feel insecure because he knows we cannot simultaneously enjoy life and have negative feelings about ourselves. Thank God, we can break out of his trap and start enjoying our blood-bought freedom and liberty.

Because we belong to God and we are in Christ, we actually have a right to be free and to enjoy our freedom. Jesus speaks of this right to be free in John 8:31–32: "If you abide in My word...you are truly My disciples. And you will know the truth [regarding salvation], and the truth will set you free [from the penalty of sin]" (AMP). And John 8:36 says, "So if the Son sets you free, you will be free indeed."

Today's verse also mentions becoming a slave (servant) of righteousness. Being a servant of righteousness is not legalistic; it is freeing. Let me ask you: Are you enjoying spiritual freedom in Jesus, or are you sacrificing your joy because you are trapped in the legalistic, rigid mindset of believing you have to please God in your own strength, punish yourself for your sin, or meet certain standards in order to be in relationship with God? If you live an inflexible life, you will not have an enjoyable life. I know this firsthand. The time came when I faced the fact that I was legalistic and rigid in my life, and though realizing this truth was hard on me emotionally, God used it to set me free.

Jesus came that we might "have and enjoy life" to the fullest, until it overflows (John 10:10 AMPC). Following a legalistic lifestyle will lead us into works—futile efforts that cause us to struggle and live in frustration. Remember, there is no bondage or burden in God. His rules (His ways for us to do things) are fulfilling and liberating. Jesus came to set us free!

Feeling guilty and condemned most of the time is not freedom. Being in mental and emotional turmoil is not freedom. Being sad and depressed is not freedom.

Have you reached the point where you are tired of trying to be in control of everything? Are you willing to give up and ask God to help you? If so, pray this prayer: "Lord, I am tired of being legalistic and complicated. I just want to have some peace and enjoy my life. So, Lord, give me the desire to do what is right in Your eyes. If You do not do what needs to be done, then it is not going to get done. I completely surrender, and I place my trust in You."

I encourage you to lay aside sin, along with the limitations and defeat of legalism. Do your best, beginning right now, to experience the joy of the freedom God makes available to you in Jesus Christ.

Things to Think About

1. In your own words, describe the joy you feel because you have been set free from sin.

2. In what ways do you need to abandon legalism or inflexible ways in order to enjoy the freedom God has given you in Christ?

CHAPTER 45

Don't Grow Tired of Doing Good

2 Thessalonians 3:13

And as for you, brothers and sisters, never tire of doing what is good.

If you ever find yourself low on joy and wanting to increase it, try doing something good. When we do good, we make others happy—and that in turn gives us joy. We can gain a fuller understanding of today's Scripture verse by looking at it in the Amplified Bible, Classic Edition, which says we are not to "become weary or lose heart in doing right [but continue in well-doing without weakening]." This teaches us that doing what is good occasionally or for a short while will not bring the breakthroughs we need when we find it necessary to persevere through various situations in life. Paul exhorts us to *continue* doing the right thing without losing heart, meaning to do it without growing tired, frustrated, or discouraged. We must do it over and over and over, and when we feel ourselves becoming weary, we should go to God, ask for His help, and wait on Him to give us fresh strength. Then we can receive His grace, which enables us to press through challenges and accomplish His will.

> The joy of Jesus was the absolute self-surrender and self-sacrifice of Himself to His Father, the joy of doing that which the Father sent Him to do.
>
> Oswald Chambers, *My Utmost for His Highest*

Doing what is good when we do not seem to get good results is difficult, but it must be done. Think of it this way: When farmers plant seeds in the ground, they must keep patient vigil over the seeds until they finally sprout and produce a harvest. This is a process that requires time and effort. If the farmers give up on the crop and stop caring for it, they will miss the joy of harvest—the good fruit of their work and perseverance.

One of Satan's favorite and often-used tactics against us as we move forward in God is to try to get us to give up. He knows that if we quit, we will not only fail to complete the assignments God has given us, but we may also be ashamed or frustrated with ourselves for not persevering. However, God teaches us to endure, persist, continue, and finish (Galatians 6:9; Hebrews 12:1). He teaches us to be long-suffering, patient, determined, and steadfast (Galatians 5:22; Psalm 37:7; Romans 8:25).

Experience has taught me that I often have to treat other people well for a long time before they begin to treat me the same way. I have to do the right thing with a right attitude sometimes long before I start getting right results. I have to persevere in doing good before good comes back to me. Just as natural seed finally takes root and a sprout begins to break through the soil, we also will see breakthrough if we continue to do good, regardless of what others do.

People frequently give up too easily. They allow themselves to be led by their emotions, meaning that when they feel they want to quit on something or someone, they simply stop making any effort. Many times, people quit just before they could have experienced breakthrough, and they miss the joys they could have known. I have learned that I can feel wrong and still choose to do what is right.

One sign of spiritual maturity is the ability to live beyond our feelings. People who are spiritually mature live by decisions made based on God's Word, not on how they feel. When we advance to this stage of growth, we are well on our way to a wonderful harvest that will leave us amazed.

Let me encourage you today: Do not give up. Persevere through difficulties, and be patient. Keep trusting in God, and keep on keeping on!

Things to Think About

1. What situation are you facing right now that requires perseverance?
2. How can you keep doing what is good and right in this situation, so that you and others eventually find joy in it?

CHAPTER 46

Set Your Mind toward Joy

Colossians 3:2 AMPC

And set your minds and keep them set on what is above (the higher things), not on the things that are on the earth.

We need to put our minds where we want our lives to be because our lives follow where our thoughts lead (Proverbs 23:7). A made-up mind is very powerful. What we think about determines the quality of our life. When we think joyful thoughts, we live a joyful life.

The Amplified Bible, Classic Edition version is the only one I know of that reads "And set your minds *and keep them set* on what is above" (emphasis mine). Setting our minds on the right thing once or twice won't do us much good, but if we set them in the right direction and keep them set—without wavering—we will live in strength and victory.

> I want to challenge you today to begin to give God the things that are on your mind that worry you. Ask Him for the grace to trust Him with the things you can't change. As you start to let go of worry, you'll experience more and more of His joy.
>
> Joyce Meyer

When Paul urges us to set our minds and keep them set "on what is above (the higher things)," he means that if we want to live a high life—a life that honors God—we cannot think about things that are low, base, common, or ungodly. Low thoughts include thinking about what you don't have instead of what you do have, and thinking about people who have things you would like and saying they don't deserve them. Jealousy, pride, anger, comparison, and judgment are low, as is holding grudges against people instead of forgiving them. Focusing on your faults instead of your strengths is low, and so is wallowing in self-pity and feeling condemned about your past mistakes.

High thinking is the opposite of low thinking. When your thoughts are set on things above, you thank God for every blessing you do have instead of complaining about what you don't have. You rejoice with others over their successes instead of being envious. You encourage people who are pursuing what you would like to do or what you would like to have instead of secretly hoping they don't get it. You choose peace over anger, humility over pride, mercy over judgment, and forgiveness over unforgiveness. You pray instead of worrying; you trust God in every situation instead of taking matters into your own hands; you stand firm in faith that God has a bright future for you instead of feeling guilty over your past. You think the best, not the worst, about everyone. As you can see, high thoughts lead to joy. There are many other ways to think high thoughts, and I believe these examples will help you know how to do that.

Once you have set your mind on something, it's important to keep it set and to not doubt yourself or become double-minded. This is how you defeat the devil on the battlefield of the mind. The apostle James says, "The one who doubts is like a wave of the sea, blown and tossed by the wind... Such a person is double-minded and unstable in all they do" (James 1:6, 8). Once you have explored your options, prayed, sought God's will, and made a decision about a matter, you can set your mind firmly on that course of action. You have to reach the point where you know that what you plan to do is the right thing and say, "My mind is made up. With God's help, this is what I'm going to do, and it will produce good results in my life." When you have a made-up mind and you are a born-again person with the Holy Spirit to help you, there is nothing you cannot do through Christ. You may not have victory overnight, but you will have it eventually if you don't give up.

Things to Think About

1. In what areas of your life do you need to set your mind toward joy and keep it set?
2. When you begin to lose your joy, what specific thoughts can you think in order to restore it?

CHAPTER 47

Deeply Rooted in God's Love

Ephesians 3:17-19

And I pray that you, being rooted and established in love, may have power, together with all the Lord's holy people, to grasp how wide and long and high and deep is the love of Christ, and to know this love that surpasses knowledge—that you may be filled to the measure of all the fullness of God.

Do you know that you can experience the love of God in a powerful, personal way and even become deeply "rooted and established" in it? When this happens, it makes you secure, just as a tree with deep roots is steady, stable, and strong, even during the fiercest storms. The deeper a tree's roots, the more difficult it is for storms to uproot and destroy it. The same principle applies to your life with God.

One of the best ways I know to become deeply rooted in God's love is to meditate on it frequently and learn to look for signs of it on a daily basis. As you become more conscious and aware of God's love at all times, you will recognize it more easily and more often. When you see it, your joy will increase as you are reminded

> *Where there is love, there is joy.*
> Mother Teresa of Calcutta

that God loves you more than you can imagine and that He is always near and active in your life.

In Romans 8:35, 38–39, Paul encourages his readers not to let anything separate them from the love of God that is found in Christ Jesus: not "tribulation, or distress, or persecution, or famine" (AMP), or anything else. When we have problems, they should drive us deeper into God, not away from Him. He is not the source of our problems; He is the answer to them. God's Word does not guarantee us a life with no trials and disappointments, but it does assure us of His love and guarantees that we will never be alone. Your worst day with Jesus will be better than your best day was without Him.

Paul doesn't want us to merely know about God's love, but also to have personal experience with it, because encounters with His love are much better than mere knowledge. Knowing God's love in this practical and personal way makes us bold in prayer, and seeing answers to our prayers helps us know even more deeply the great and endless love of God. There is never one moment in our lives when God doesn't love us. He reveals His love to us in many ways, but sadly, we may be unaware of it, or even worse, we may become so accustomed to the many things that God does for us that we begin to take them for granted.

By His grace, God always provides everything we need, and He never asks us to do for anyone else what He has not first done for us. He gives us mercy and asks us to give it to others, He forgives us and asks us to forgive, and He is kind and asks us to be the same. He loves us unconditionally and asks us to love in the same way. Always remember that the more time you spend receiving and abiding in God's love, the more you will be able to let it flow through you to other people.

Knowing that God loves us gives us joy. It also fills us with confidence and boldness and allows us to pray without fear. God wants to do more for us than we can ask or imagine (Ephesians 3:20). The more God does for us, the more we are able to do for others. I am not speaking only of material things we ask for, but also of qualities such as peace and joy. The more peace we receive from God, the more peace we can bring into each situation we encounter. Similarly, the more joy we have in our hearts, the more we have to share with others.

Things to Think About

1. Do you struggle to consistently know that God loves you no matter what your circumstances look like? Explain.
2. Have you experienced God's love, and do you see signs of His love in your daily life? What are they?

CHAPTER 48

The Joy of Living in the Present

Philippians 3:12-14

Not that I have already obtained all this, or have already arrived at my goal, but I press on to take hold of that for which Christ Jesus took hold of me. Brothers and sisters, I do not consider myself yet to have taken hold of it. But one thing I do: Forgetting what is behind and straining toward what is ahead, I press on toward the goal to win the prize for which God has called me heavenward in Christ Jesus.

We do not see the word *joy* in today's Scripture passage, but when we read it we can sense the joy Paul felt in knowing Christ. He wants to make clear to his readers that he has not yet reached his goal and that he is still moving toward all that God has for him. While sharing our victories with others can be beneficial, it is also good to share our journeys, admitting that we are not yet where we ultimately hope to be. Our victory stories come after our journeys are complete, but to share only our victories without being honest about the challenges, difficulties, and pain of the journey does not help people who are hurting. In fact, it may confuse them and make them wonder why others always seem to be enjoying victory while they are still in a difficult place with painful circumstances.

If we fear being vulnerable, we will often pretend everything is wonderful when, in reality, we are struggling and hurting. Paul didn't do that. He shared many victories, but did not exclude his weaknesses and struggles from his writing.

> *Joy does not simply happen to us. We have to choose joy and keep choosing it every day.*
>
> Henri Nouwen

One key to Paul's joy was that he had the ability to put the past behind him. Paul states that his one goal is forgetting the past and pressing toward the full will of God. Paul knew he could not make progress today if he held on to yesterday's mistakes. This is a very powerful truth, which is important for us to realize. Today holds possibilities for those who embrace it and look earnestly for what it may hold for them. Today is very important because once it is gone, you can never get it back again. Don't waste it worrying about the mistakes of the past.

Being able to let go of the past and fully embrace the present while looking forward to the future is a guaranteed way to increase the joy in your life. If you were asked what the most important day in your life had been, what would you say? Some might say it was the day they married, or graduated from college, or had their first child. While all of those are wonderful occasions, none of those answers would be correct, because the most important day of any of our lives is today. Many important days hold memories we cherish, but nothing compares to the importance of today, because today matters more than you may realize.

The Old Testament prophet Isaiah speaks for God when he says: "Forget the former things; do not dwell on the past. See, I am doing a new thing! Now it springs up; do you not perceive it?" (Isaiah 43:18–19).

If we do not let go of the past, we will miss the new things that God is doing in our lives. Another way to say this is that if we do not let go of yesterday, we cannot take hold of today. Paul knew this to be true. If anyone had reason to regret the past, Paul did. He had persecuted Christians, but he received God's forgiveness and grace, and he effectively put his past behind him. The same God who showed grace, mercy, and forgiveness to Paul is eager to show grace, mercy, and forgiveness to you. Your life, like Paul's, can be totally transformed. You can follow Paul's example of "forgetting what is behind" as you press on toward all God has for you now and in the future.

Things to Think About

1. If guilt and shame have kept you stuck in the past, how has this affected you?
2. Will you ask God today to help you accept His forgiveness and to help you move forward so you can enjoy the wonderful future He has for you?

CHAPTER 49

The Right Kind of Confidence

Philippians 3:4-7

I myself have reasons for such confidence. If someone else thinks they have reasons to put confidence in the flesh, I have more: circumcised on the eighth day, of the people of Israel, of the tribe of Benjamin, a Hebrew of Hebrews; in regard to the law, a Pharisee; as for zeal, persecuting the church; as for righteousness based on the law, faultless. But whatever were gains to me I now consider loss for the sake of Christ.

Putting no confidence in ourselves is easy if we feel we have nothing about which to be confident. But if we feel we have natural reasons for self-confidence, we may struggle to learn that placing our confidence in anyone other than Christ is foolish.

> God's gifts, through Christ, fill the treasures of the soul, they fill its joys.
> Matthew Henry, Complete Commentary (John 16:24)

God wants us to be totally dependent upon Him, not to be independent or self-sufficient. Jesus teaches that we are the branches and He is the vine, and He urges us to abide (live, dwell, remain) in Him. He says that those who abide in Him will bear much fruit (John 15:4–5).

Think about a branch that has been broken off a vine. On the first day after it is disconnected, it has plenty of plump, life-filled leaves. Three days later, the leaves are crispy around the edges and you can easily see that they are dying. This represents what happens to us when we try to be independent of God and dependent on ourselves or others. When we are not connected to Him, we experience a loss of fulfillment and success. Like the leaves in the example, we will see signs of drying up and a diminishing of our quality of life.

Putting our confidence in God does not mean we should not try to do anything for ourselves or to fail to fulfill the responsibilities He gives us, but we should do them while totally leaning and relying on Jesus. He does want us to mature spiritually and take responsibility for ourselves, but always with His will in mind. He wants us to admit that we need His help in order to succeed instead of seeing ourselves as the source of our successes.

Self-reliance is rooted in a need to feel proud of what we have accomplished, but we must avoid such pride and the temptation to take credit for our accomplishments. We hear people say, "I'm a self-made person." This means that they think they have the type of life they do because they have worked hard and created it without anyone's help. The world applauds the "self-made" person, but self-generated, worldly success saddens God because it prevents people from receiving from Him the divine help they could have enjoyed. No matter how great people may think their lives are without God, life is always much, much better with Him.

A person may achieve success in the world's eyes and have no peace or joy, which are the true marks of success. People may have money, but they have used others to get it. They have missed the joy of truly loving people and helping them succeed. Many who appear to be the most successful people in the world are actually very unhappy.

Jesus says that those who are weary and overburdened can come to Him and He will give them rest for their souls (Matthew 11:28). This invitation is, I believe, directed to all the self-reliant, self-confident people who are worn out from trying to do things on their own.

Paul had a great deal to be self-confident about, and you

can read about his credentials in Philippians 3:5–6. He had been proud of his hard-earned accomplishments until the day he met Christ and experienced His grace. That day Paul began to see his life differently. He realized that nothing he did could be of any value unless Jesus was first in his life at all times and in all things. The same is true for us. Learning to find our confidence in Christ alone and give Him glory for everything we accomplish and enjoy is a key to joy.

Things to Think About

1. Have you ever felt spiritually dry? If you have drifted away from Christ, how can you reconnect with Him?
2. What is the difference between experiencing true, godly joy and enjoying worldly success?

CHAPTER 50

Enjoy Your Preparation

2 Timothy 2:15

Do your best to present yourself to God as one approved, a worker who does not need to be ashamed and who correctly handles the word of truth.

In today's scripture, Paul writes to Timothy, encouraging him to prepare thoroughly to fulfill God's call on his life. The lesson in this verse for each of us—whether we are in full-time ministry or not—is that we should do our very best to be prepared to fulfill God's plan for us. God Himself does not do anything without first being ready for it, and He is careful not to release us to do His work or fulfill the purposes He has for our lives without adequate preparation.

> You have made known to me the paths of life; you will fill me with joy in your presence.
>
> Acts 2:28

No matter what God desires for you to do with your life—perhaps to be a teacher, a doctor, a computer programmer, a stay-at-home parent, an athlete, an artist, a pastor, a Bible teacher, or a law enforcement officer—you will need to prepare to know what to do and how to do it. Training will be a stepping-stone to success.

Your process of becoming ready for all that God has for you may mean going to Bible college, attending a university or an academy, or receiving some other kind of formal equipping in the field God has chosen for you. It may also mean spending a few years working under someone else's authority so you know how to handle your life and your calling in the future. It could mean working at a job you do not particularly like for a boss you are not very fond of, or working hours that are not convenient. It could also mean spending some years in which your basic needs are met but you definitely are not living in abundance. You are trusting God for prosperity, but He is teaching you how to handle it when you get it.

When I use the word *prosperity*, I am not referring only to financial resources. Money may be part of prosperity, but we can also prosper in our souls. In fact, in 3 John 2, the apostle John writes: "Beloved, I pray that you may prosper in all things and be in health, just as your soul prospers" (NKJV). Prosperity in your soul includes love, peace, joy, faith, and enjoying what you do each day. Many people desire to prosper, but not all want to prepare to prosper.

Preparation is not limited to the job or vocation to which God calls you. It takes place in a lot of different settings and has many different phases. Even in the later years of your life, preparation is important as you approach the challenges and transitions of aging.

Each phase we go through in our preparation is important. There are lessons to be learned at every step. We must "graduate," so to speak, from each phase or level into the next one, and this comes after we prove ourselves on the current level. Between all of these stages of preparation, there is a lot of waiting.

Unless we learn to wait well, we will be unhappy and frustrated, and our waiting periods will be difficult instead of hopeful and joyful. I want to be joyful in every season of life, and I'm sure you do too. When we can go through any situation, for any length of time, with joy, we are stronger and happier, and we inspire the people around us to be joyful too.

I hope you will enjoy every aspect of your trip through life! When you reach a time of preparation, realize that you are in training and becoming equipped for something great in God's Kingdom.

Things to Think About

1. Consider God's call on your life. What steps do you need to take in order to be prepared to fulfill it?
2. What changes can you make in your life so that you will find greater joy in the seasons of preparation through which God leads you?

Do you have a real relationship with Jesus?

God loves you! He created you to be a special, unique, one-of-a-kind individual, and He has a specific purpose and plan for your life. And through a personal relationship with your Creator—God—you can discover a way of life that will truly satisfy your soul.

No matter who you are, what you've done, or where you are in your life right now, God's love and grace are greater than your sin—your mistakes. Jesus willingly gave His life so you can receive forgiveness from God and have new life in Him. He's just waiting for you to invite Him to be your Savior and Lord.

If you are ready to commit your life to Jesus and follow Him, all you have to do is ask Him to forgive your sins and give you a fresh start in the life you are meant to live. Begin by praying this prayer...

Lord Jesus, thank You for giving Your life for me and forgiving me of my sins so I can have a personal relationship with You. I am sincerely sorry for the mistakes I've made, and I know I need You to help me live right.

Your Word says in Romans 10:9, "If you declare with your mouth, 'Jesus is Lord,' and believe in your heart that God raised him from the dead, you will be saved" (NIV). I believe You are the Son of God and confess You as my Savior and Lord. Take me just as I am, and work in my heart, making me the person You want me to be. I want to live for You, Jesus, and I am so grateful that You are giving me a fresh start in my new life with You today.

I love You, Jesus!

It's so amazing to know that God loves us so much! He wants to have a deep, intimate relationship with us that grows every day as we spend time with Him in prayer and Bible study. And we want to encourage you in your new life in Christ.

Please visit joycemeyer.org/salvation to request Joyce's book *A New Way of Living*, which is our gift to you. We also have other free resources online to help you make progress in pursuing everything God has for you.

Congratulations on your fresh start in your life in Christ! We hope to hear from you soon.

Joyce Meyer is one of the world's leading practical Bible teachers. A *New York Times* bestselling author, Joyce's books have helped millions of people find hope and restoration through Jesus Christ. Joyce's program, *Enjoying Everyday Life*, airs around the world on television, radio, and online to millions worldwide in more than 100 languages. Through Joyce Meyer Ministries, Joyce teaches internationally on a number of topics with a particular focus on how the Word of God applies to our everyday lives. Her candid communication style allows her to share openly and practically about her experiences so others can apply what she has learned to their lives.

Joyce has authored more than 135 books, which have been translated into more than 160 languages, and over 37 million of her books have been distributed free of charge worldwide. Bestsellers include *Power Thoughts*; *The Confident Woman*; *Look Great, Feel Great*; *Starting Your Day Right*; *Ending Your Day Right*; *Approval Addiction*; *How to Hear from God*; *Beauty for Ashes*; and *Battlefield of the Mind*.

Joyce's passion to help hurting people is foundational to the vision of Hand of Hope, the missions arm of Joyce

Meyer Ministries. Hand of Hope provides worldwide humanitarian outreaches such as feeding programs, medical and dental care, critical relief after natural disasters, human trafficking intervention and rehabilitation, and much more—always sharing the love and gospel of Christ.

JOYCE MEYER MINISTRIES

U.S. & FOREIGN OFFICE
ADDRESSES

Joyce Meyer Ministries
P.O. Box 655
Fenton, MO 63026
USA
(636) 349-0303

Joyce Meyer Ministries—Canada
P.O. Box 7700
Vancouver, BC V6B 4E2
Canada
(800) 868-1002

Joyce Meyer Ministries—Australia
Locked Bag 77
Mansfield Delivery Centre
Queensland 4122
Australia
(07) 3349 1200

Joyce Meyer Ministries—England
P.O. Box 1549
Windsor SL4 1GT
United Kingdom
01753 831102

Joyce Meyer Ministries—South Africa
P.O. Box 5
Cape Town 8000
South Africa
(27) 21-701-1056

Joyce Meyer Ministries—Francophonie
29 avenue Maurice Chevalier
77330 Ozoir la Ferriere
France

Joyce Meyer Ministries—Germany
Postfach 761001
22060 Hamburg
Germany
+49 (0)40 / 88 88 4 11 11

Joyce Meyer Ministries—Netherlands
Lorenzlaan 14
7002 HB Doetinchem
+31 657 555 9789

Joyce Meyer Ministries—Russia
P.O. Box 789
Moscow 101000
Russia
+7 (495) 727-14-68

Straight Talk
Strength for Each Day
Teenagers Are People Too!
Trusting God Day by Day
The Word, the Name, the Blood
Woman to Woman
You Can Begin Again
Your Battles Belong to the Lord*

JOYCE MEYER SPANISH TITLES

Auténtica y única (Authentically, Uniquely You)
Belleza en lugar de cenizas (Beauty for Ashes)
Buena salud, buena vida (Good Health, Good Life)
Cambia tus palabras, cambia tu vida (Change Your Words, Change Your Life)
El campo de batalla de la mente (Battlefield of the Mind)
Cómo envejecer sin avejentarse (How to Age without Getting Old)
Como formar buenos habitos y romper malos habitos (Making Good Habits, Breaking Bad Habits)
La conexión de la mente (The Mind Connection)
Dios no está enojado contigo (God Is Not Mad at You)
La dosis de aprobación (The Approval Fix)
Efesios: Comentario biblico (Ephesians: Biblical Commentary)
Empezando tu día bien (Starting Your Day Right)
Hágalo con miedo (Do It Afraid)
Hazte un favor a ti mismo…perdona (Do Yourself a Favor…Forgive)
Madre segura de sí misma (The Confident Mom)
Momentos de quietud con Dios (Quiet Times with God Devotional)
Pensamientos de poder (Power Thoughts)
El poder del agradecimiento (The Power of Thank You)
Sanidad para el alma de una mujer (Healing the Soul of a Woman)
Santiago: Comentario bíblico (James: Biblical Commentary)
Sobrecarga (Overload)
Sus batallas son del Señor (Your Battles Belong to the Lord)
Termina bien tu día (Ending Your Day Right)
Usted puede comenzar de nuevo (You Can Begin Again)
Viva valientemente (Living Courageously)

* Study Guide available for this title

BOOKS BY DAVE MEYER

Life Lines